CIVILITY
AND CITIZENSHIP
IN LIBERAL DEMOCRATIC
SOCIETIES

World Social Systems

Morton A. Kaplan
General Editor

LIBERAL DEMOCRATIC SOCIETIES

Roger Michener and Edward Shils Editors

Civility and Citizenship
Edward Banfield

Morality and Religion
Gordon L. Anderson and Morton A. Kaplan

The Mass Media
Stanley Rothman

The Balance of Freedom: Economy, Law and Learning
Roger Michener

Nationality, Nationalism, and Patriotism
Roger Michener

Work and Employment
David Marsland

Liberal Democracy in Non-Western Civilizations
Dennis Austin

THE SOVIET UNION
AND THE CHALLENGE OF THE FUTURE

Alexander Shtromas and Morton A. Kaplan Editors

Vol. 1 *The Soviet System: Stasis and Change*

Vol. 2 *Economy and Society*

Vol. 3 *Ideology, Culture, and Nationality*

Vol. 4 *Russia and the World*

CHINA IN A NEW ERA

Ilpyong J. Kim Series Editor

Chinese Defense and Foreign Policy
June Teufel Dreyer

Chinese Economic Policy
Bruce Reynolds

Chinese Politics from Mao to Deng
Victor C. Falkenheim

Professors World Peace Academy Books

CIVILITY AND CITIZENSHIP IN LIBERAL DEMOCRATIC SOCIETIES

Edited by
Edward C. Banfield

A PWPA Book

PARAGON HOUSE
New York

Published in the United States by
Professors World Peace Academy
4 West 43 Street
New York, New York 10036

Distributed by Paragon House Publishers
90 Fifth Avenue
New York, New York 10011

A Professors World Peace Academy Book

The Professors World Peace Academy (PWPA) is an international association of
professors, scholars and academics from diverse backgrounds, devoted to issues
concerning world peace. PWPA sustains a program of conferences and publications on topics in peace studies, area and cultural studies, national and international development, education, economics and international relations.

Library of Congress Catalog-in-Publication Data

Civility and citizenship in liberal democratic societies / edited by Edward C.
Banfield.
    175 p.
Based on papers presented at the Fourth International Conference of the
Professors World Peace Academy, held in London, England, Aug. 1989.
    "A PWPA Book."
    Includes index.
    ISBN 0-89226-104-8 (HC). — ISBN 0-89226-105-6 (pbk.)
    1. Democracy — Congresses. 2. Civil rights — Congresses.
    3. Citizenship — Congresses. 4. Liberalism — Congresses.
    5. Political participation — Congresses. I. Banfield, Edward C. II. Professors
World Peace Academy. International Conference (4th: 1989: London, England)
JC423.C57   1991
321.8 — dc20

                                             91-11662
                                           CIP

TABLE OF CONTENTS

CONTRIBUTORS

Katherine Auspitz, author of *The Radical Bourgeoisie*, is Personnel Director for the City of Somerville, Mass., and writes about modern European history and politics.

Edward C. Banfield is the George D. Markham Professor of Government Emeritus at Harvard University.

Robert A. Goldwin is a resident scholar and director of constitutional studies at the American Enterprise Institute. His most recent book is *Why Blacks, Women, and Jews Are Not Mentioned in the Constitution and other Unorthodox Views*.

Elie Kedourie holds the Chair of Politics in the University of London. He is a Fellow of the British Academy and the author of many books, including *Nationalism*, first published in 1960.

Charles R. Kesler is Associate Professor of Government at Claremont McKenna College. He is the editor of *Saving the Revolution, the Federalist Papers and the American Founding*.

Clifford Orwin is a Fellow of St. Michael's College and Professor of Political Science at the University of Toronto. He has published widely on both classical and modern political thought.

Edward Shils, professor of sociology and social thought at the University of Chicago and honorary fellow of Peterhouse, Cambridge, is the editor of *Minerva: A Review of Science, Learning, and Policy*.

Myron Weiner is professor of political science at the Massachusetts Institute of Technology and director of the Center for International Studies there. He has written extensively on the politics of India and is currently writing a book on international migration.

James Q. Wilson, Collins Professor of Management and Public Policy at the University of California Los Angeles, has written extensively on crime. His most recent book is *Bureaucracy*.

SERIES EDITORS' FOREWORD

Liberal democratic societies, as patterns of political, economic and social arrangements, would seem to be vindicated against their detractors. Until recently Marxism in its various forms and other proponents of single party states and centrally planned economies appeared to offer realistic and allegedly beneficial alternatives to liberal democracy. Events in China, the Soviet Union, Eastern Europe, and the Third World have so reduced the persuasiveness of these arguments that there are no readily apparent alternatives to liberal democratic societies.

Nevertheless, the discomfitures and embarrassments of single party states should not be regarded as a justification for complacency. We should be appreciative of the merits of liberal democratic societies, but we should be aware of their shortcomings, in light of their own ideals, and of the dangers to which they are liable.

The purpose of the present series of books is to take stock of and to assess, in an historical perspective, the most central achievements and shortcomings of liberal democratic societies, and to encourage thought on their maintenance and improvement.

Not only do we seek to delineate some of these main lines of historical development of the variant forms of liberal democracy, but we also seek to discern certain fundamental postulates that are common to these institutions and processes. In this way, we hope to define more clearly the liberal democratic ideal and its limits. We wish to learn where the practice falls short of the ideal or deforms it. We wish to form an estimate of the destructive forces within the liberal democratic ideal itself and of their potentialities for causing its deterioration or its collapse. We wish above all to learn how these destructive potentialities may be averted.

CIVILITY AND CITIZENSHIP

This series insists on the bond between liberalism and democracy. Liberalism and democracy are two distinguishable components of present day liberal democratic societies. Their combination into a particular form of society is a great achievement but it is also a source of difficult problems. For instance, can these societies reconcile the fundamental conflict between minimizing governmental authority and intrusiveness and the democratic demand for more governmental activities and greater governmental provision of welfare services? What are the consequences of some of the institutions of liberal democratic society for the daily life of the individual in his or her private sphere? These questions, and others like them, constitute a continuing challenge for the present and successor generations. These books are devised to assist in the understanding of that challenge.

Roger Michener
Edward Shils

INTRODUCTORY NOTE

Edward C. Banfield

The papers brought together here address a crucially important but little regarded question: How do civility and citizenship, aspects of the individual's attachment to a liberal democratic society, affect the nature and future of that society? They were written for the Fourth International Conference of the Professors World Peace Academy which met in London in August 1989. In the words of its organizers, the purpose of the Conference was to "take stock of and to assess, in an historical perspective, the most central achievements and shortcomings of liberal democratic societies." The Conference met in eleven panels; six of the papers printed here were delivered to the panel on Civility and Citizenship; two, those by Professors Kedourie and Weiner, were commissioned later.

The contributors to the panel were not chosen for any agreement that might be presumed to exist among them, apart from devotion to liberal democratic institutions. On the contrary. It was taken for granted that full agreement was neither possible nor desirable and that the purposes of the Conference would be best served if opposing views were vigorously presented. As may be seen from the Note on Contributors, the writers, all but one an American, come from various specialties within social science and political philosophy.

When in the early summer of 1989 the first papers reached the editor, hundreds of thousands of brave men and women were standing shoulder to shoulder in the public squares of China and Eastern Europe holding placards that demanded in one language or another DEMOCRACY and FREEDOM. Here were people who understood all too well the meaning of tyranny and oppression.

Would that understanding enable them to find their way to democracy and freedom? One hoped so and hoped also that the papers written for the Conference might help them in this. But the painful fact is, as the papers in many ways explain, that liberal democracy is by its nature always of slow growth, depending as it must upon widespread acceptance of certain ideas, sentiments, and habits as well as the existence of certain practices and institutions, both economic and political, the establishment of which requires much time—centuries perhaps—as well as favorable external circumstances and which are never so firmly established as to be beyond danger of decay or subversion. Much as one wishes that the papers presented here might offer guidance to those who now glimpse dawn after a long night of tyranny it would be fatuous to offer this to them as a how-to-do-it manual.

The most we can hope to do is to point to some of the hazards that threaten liberal democracy where it exists. We who live in liberal democracies are too apt to accept them as we do the sunshine: a blessing that has befallen us. The papers collected here are reminders of the fragility of a good political order, of the complexity of the circumstances that produce and maintain such an order, and of the uncertainties that follow upon even wise and virtuous actions.

For the purposes of this Introductory Note it will suffice to draw attention to some of the questions upon which discussion of these matters must turn.

One such question is about the nature of liberal democracy. Everyone knows that democracy is rule by the people. It is tempting to suppose that where the people rule there can be no tyranny. But history and reflection tell us that this is not so: a majority may tyrannize cruelly over a minority. What we want is not majority rule simply, but majority rule plus the protection of certain rights that pertain to individuals. This is the difference between democracy and liberal democracy: in the latter there is a private sphere into which the governing authority may not intrude no matter how large the majority behind it.

In a liberal democracy the citizen is one who has the right to vote and who therefore shares the obligation to protect the rights pertaining to the private sphere. Citizenship implies a sense of shared responsibility for the conduct of the regime; a regime is fully liberal but less than fully democratic if rights are protected but significant numbers of persons are denied, or decline to accept and exercise, the duties of citizenship. It will be found that by this test the number of nations that approach the ideal of liberal democracy—that are at once very liberal and very democratic—is painfully small and that the most liberal are not those in which citizenship is most widely held and exercised. A private sphere must be well marked by boundaries which clearly and authoritatively specify the nature and extent of individual rights. There must, in other words, be a constitution, written or unwritten, which defines the limits beyond which government may not go without infringing upon the private sphere.

This, however, is not enough: that there is a well marked boundary does not mean that it will not be overstepped. A regime is not a liberal democracy unless there are institutions—laws, courts, and police—capable both of finding when rights have been violated and of putting a stop to their violation. Such institutions can exist and function only as public opinion permits and requires. In a liberal democracy one who contemplates violating the law must know in advance that if push comes to shove his effort must fail because public opinion will not stand for it to succeed.

It follows that in a liberal democracy public opinion must value the protection of the private sphere above all else, a condition hard to meet for it means that no belief or attachment—not religion, not ideology, not tribal or ethnic association—can take precedence over the protection of individual rights, including those the exercise of which may be blatantly offensive to most members of the society. This amounts to saying that what the majority holds sacred may on occasion have to be subordinated to what it deems demonic.

Obviously a liberal democratic society can never be wholly at peace within itself. There will always be persons who out of devotion to some supposed good that they hold higher than the peace and order, perhaps even the preservation, of the society are bent on actions that will destroy the consensual basis of the society. The example of the American Civil War reminds us that irreconcilable conflicts may demand settlement by force of arms.

If a liberal democratic society is to continue as such there must be widely respected institutions, practices, and modes of thought that encourage or demand the making of concessions where necessary to preserve the degree of harmony without which the society could not continue as a going concern. The obligation of the citizen to obey the law is one such safeguard of order. The idea of civic virtue is another. Civility, the culturally ingrained willingness to tolerate behavior that is in some degree offensive, is yet another.

The sharper the conflict within a society the greater the need for voluntary restraint, i.e., civility, on all sides. If peace and order, let alone good feeling, are to be preserved the parties in contention, however strenuously they bargain, must not lose sight of the danger of destroying the bargaining process altogether by making demands or refusing concessions that the other side will deem absolutely unacceptable. A shared concern for the preservation of the bargaining process must be paramount however sharp the disagreements.

Are there not some principles that should be insisted upon even though the heavens fall? Decent people will agree that there are. But they will want to ponder very deeply before they risk the destruction of one great good for the sake of another. They must keep in mind that if the liberal principle permits the propagation of error it also permits the propagation of competing truth, something an opposed principle does not.

ONE

CIVILITY AND CIVIL SOCIETY

Edward Shils

I

The attitude and ethos that distinguish the politics of a civil society is civility, i.e., a solicitude for the interest of the whole society, a concern for the common good. The civil person, when he has to decide and act in a situation in which there is conflict, thinks primarily of the civil society as the object of his obligations, not of the members of his family, or his village, or his party, or his ethnic group, or his social class, or his occupation.

Civil society and liberal democracy overlap but are not identical. Civil society comprises the institutions of liberal democracy but it also comprises a pattern of judgment, viz. civility, without which these institutions cannot flourish. I do not think that any society can be entirely a civil society, but when civility and the relations it sustains are lacking, it is scarcely possible for civil society to exist at all. Some measure of civility is indispensable to the maintenance of liberal institutions. If there is no civil society of the sort that I delineate here, the government is subject to no higher authority, to no rules which transcend its positive laws. A totalitarian society is the antithesis of civil society.

Civility was not invented by liberal or democratic social philosophers nor did the idea of civility emerge for the first time in the institutional practices of the more or less liberal societies of the nineteenth century and the more or less democratic institutions which joined them later. Civil society corresponds to liberal democratic society in its political aspects and to the pluralistic society of voluntary associations and private corporations on the other. Civil society entails the freedom of contract and the market economy; in this aspect, the idea of civility is also closely dependent on a fundamental feature of "civil society" as Hegel conceived it: namely, the private ownership of property in the market economy. The private ownership of property and the freedom of contract and the organization of the market economy around them, are necessary conditions for civility in society. Seen in the crudest terms, civility and the market seem to be antithetical to each other—one altruistic, the other egoistic, the one inclusive, the other exclusive—but in fact they are mutually dependent. The very anonymity of the market, its relative disregard for the primordial and personal, is a necessary condition of the extension of the collective self-consciousness to the inclusion of unknown and unseen persons. (The hierarchical system of self-alleged "planned economies" has turned out to be inimical to civility, as well as economically ruinous.)

Of course, some restrictions on the right of use and disposition of private property is, up to a point difficult to determine, compatible with civility. But past that point, such restrictions have been damaging to civility. The abolition of private property in communist countries was thought to be an indispensable condition of the full development of an inclusively civil society. It turned out to be diametrically the opposite. It made impossible the formation of independence of judgment, which was forced into secrecy or extirpated; it prevented entirely the free expression of independent judgment. It abolished the institutions of civil society. It rendered the rulers of communist societies among the least civil in the his-tory of the world, certainly since the beginning of modern times.

A liberal democratic society is a society of an inclusive collective self-consciousness. Of course, any society has some measure of collective self-consciousness, a minimum of civility which might be found from time to time in the circle of counsellors and scholars around the ruler in monarchies and empires, although the institutions of civil society have only a very rudimentary existence in such societies.

2

There is an inherent consensual element in collective self-consciousness—at least over the part of the population which participates in it. Collective self-consciousness becomes civil not only when it is shared or participated in by a large part of the population, but also when it assigns at least a minimum of dignity to the various sectors of the population which it comprehends. (The minimum income, for example, must be high enough to acknowledge in each of the various sectors of its recipients an essential moral dignity. Beyond that minimum of moral dignity, there might be acknowledged differences in value but what is important is the inclusiveness of the referent in the collective consciousness.)

Now this kind of comprehensive, even if unequal, awareness of nearly the whole population of the society is a crucial property of modern society. Centers in the past never thought much about peripheries except to keep them quiet, obedient and productive of foodstuffs and military manpower.

Modern liberal and then liberal democratic societies modified this markedly. The idea of equality of both center and periphery before the law, restriction of the powers of the central authority to imprison at will individuals, especially from the peripheries, the freedom of critics of the existing center to criticize it and to attempt to modify its patterns and practices, the development of institutions to represent, through the extended franchise and through consultation, the majority of the adult male and later the entire adult male and female population, are a few of the indications of the extension of the collective self-consciousness of the center. There has been a simultaneous and corresponding extension of the society-wide collective self-consciousness to the peripheries leading to their partial amalgamation into their larger society. These developments have been the products of and the conditions for the growth of civility in modern liberal democratic societies.

II

Civility in private life and civility in the face-to-face relations of participants in public life are not essentially different from each other. Good manners are a feature—unfortunately not a universally realized feature—of the direct contacts of individuals in each other's presence or at a distance through writing, telephonic communications, etc. Good manners might be highly elaborated, conventional or even idiosyncratic; they express respect or deference and avoid offensiveness. Good nature or temperamental amiability ("natural good manners") also restrict offensiveness.

There is not enough good nature or temperamental amiability in any society to permit it to dispense with good manners. Good manners are like uniforms and discipline which hide slovenliness, poor taste and unpleasing eccentricity. Good manners repress the expression of ill nature but not invariably.

In political and public institutions, good manners, i.e., civility in the sense of courtesy, permit the collaboration of persons of diverse and often inimical dispositions. A wise politician, Sir William Harcourt, once said, according to T. S. Eliot, "the survival of a parliamentary system required a constant 'dining with the opposition.'"[1] In legislative bodies which practice the politics of interest, antagonists can frequently work together easily because they are courteous towards each other, even when the realization of the intentions of one of the parties is incompatible with the realization of the intentions of the other parties. Their incompatibility notwithstanding, the contending individuals remain in courteous relations with each other. Sometimes even the practitioners of ideological politics develop civil qualities in their relations with those who, in accordance with the fervently held convictions of the ideological politicians, are doomed to go down in a final struggle.

Nevertheless, good manners in direct relationships of individuals in the public sphere are not civility. Poor manners might aggravate incivility or be a part of it. Good manners, courtesy, temperate speech in face-to-face relationships, cannot be identical with the civility which is a part of civil society. In contemporary liberal democratic societies, even the smallest of which contains about five million persons, face-to-face relationships occupy very small zones of any society. Altogether they cover only a small part of the images and relationships which are integral features of the constitution of the entire society. The larger the society in territory and numbers, the smaller the fraction of relationships conducted in face-to-face situations. In such societies, political collaboration and contention and the making of political decisions are very intensively carried on, in situations in which allies and antagonists see each other face-to-face, but the contentions and decisions refer to and affect parts of the society which the politicians do not see and with which they are only in very infrequent contact, and then only with a tiny minority of the persons referred to and affected. Furthermore, those persons who are in relationship to each other face-to-face make up, for every member of the society, only a small part of the politically active population. With the large majority, the civility of good manners and public civility have very different objects. Their good or poor manners in their immediate dealings with other persons make a difference in the quality of the daily life of the members of society but they are not directly important in politics. The referents of public civility in the collective self-consciousness of any sector of society are far more widely dispersed than are the individuals who are the objects of private civility or good manners in face-to-face relationships. Relationships with anonymous persons and classes or categories of anonymous persons over large distances are major features of liberal democracy in large societies. The public civility of those remote peripheries in their orientation towards centers of society do indeed make a considerable difference to the political order. They sustain civil society.

In a liberal democratic society in which literacy and affluence are widespread and the technology of communications makes possible and stimulates a widespread attention to and interest in the center and participation in an inclusive collective self-consciousness, political activity is not confined to a tiny minority of the head of government, cabinet members, legislators, and high officials in the government and to publicists, lobbyists, and agitators. Even though many individuals do not vote, very large numbers including "non-voters" have opinions which they express and their opinions are often markedly touched with strong emotions. Public opinion polls have given prominence to a type of political participation which was previously lacking; it is a participation which makes desires known through means other than direct communication through speaking or writing. Experienced politicians in liberal.democratic societies often have the gift of apprehending the views of their "silent" constituents. These "silent views" are also a form of political participation; I call it "participation by emanation." It is fostered by participation in the collective self-consciousness of the civil society. It is a bond between the representatives and the represented; it binds both of them. Such "participation by emanation" has never been wholly absent in liberal democracy. It is the matrix of representation.

III

Any large society which is not simply a system of imperial rule over small, largely self-contained, primordial societies, but in which the society is more or less coextensive with the territory, is inevitably a differentiated society, differentiated not only in the numerous primordial societies, which retain their own traditions to a considerable extent, but also by a division of labor (insofar as there is an exchange or market economy) and stratification of property ownership, political power and social status. Each sector of a differentiated society has "interests," i.e., ends, actually conceived, or potential, which are frequently in conflict with the "interests" of the other sectors of society. The conflicting parties see that their own advantage would be endangered by an increase in the advantage of the others. This is bound to happen when desires, in the aggregate, exceed the supply of the objects which would satisfy those desires. Conflicts are therefore inevitable; even where there is peace or harmony within a society, the conflicts are potentialities; where they are experienced as conflicts, they may be suppressed by the more powerful or they may be open. All large, differentiated open societies stand in need of civility; they must contain a large zone of civil society or they are in danger of severe conflict and disorder.

Civility is an attitude and a mode of action which attempts to strike a balance between conflicting demands and conflicting interests. Liberal democracy is especially in need of the virtue of civility because liberal democracy is more prone to bring latent conflicts into actuality.

Liberal democracy has opened the political field to the demands of all sectors of society and it has tended to attribute legitimacy to the demands of those classes and groups who previously had no continuously open way to give voice to their demands. Liberalism provided the institutions through representative government and the prerequisite public liberties through which such demands could be made public; democracy brought into those institutions the classes whose demands were unspoken in public or, when spoken, were unheeded by others. No society has ever had a complete "harmony of interests." Liberal democracy has made the disharmony of interests more visible and audible to all other parts of the society. The sight of interests, asserted and realized, has heightened the self-consciousness not only of the exponents of those interests but of those who are, within their own society, spectators of these conflicts. The growth of wealth, the increased desires of the electorate, their increased awareness of government and their increased turning to government for the satisfaction of these desires, and the increased readiness of governments to attempt to satisfy those desires, have combined to make it appear that their demands are realizable. The belief in the realizability of a demand encourages the further articulation of demands and more forceful insistence on their gratification.

The freedom of the press and of assembly and petition have given more opportunity for demands to be expressed in public and to become known to most parts of society. Their expression has encouraged the emergence of new demands from previously relatively undemanding parts of the population.

Intellectuals, with their hostility towards their respective societies and particularly towards the centers of those societies and their belief in the rightness of the demands of any group at the periphery against the center, have given resonance to demands and have thereby fostered their intensity and insistence.

There has been an antinomy at the heart of liberal democracy throughout the period since World War II. On the one side, demanding groups seek satisfaction for their demands through the exertions of government. On the other, since the demands are insatiable, indeed have grown with their practical satisfaction, the capacity of the government to satisfy those demands is diminished relative to the demands. Therefore, the authority of government is put into question because the legitimacy of government is to a large extent dependent on its effectiveness in realizing its intentions. Government is regarded almost exclusively as an instrument for the satisfaction of demands. Its legitimacy is not acknowledged unless it satisfies particular parochial demands. The press—the printed press and television—contributes to the undermining of the legitimacy of government. It denies to governments the prerogatives of sovereign power to exercise discretion in the choice of alternatives in their compromise and to refuse demands out of concern for the common good. It strengthens the tendency towards interest politics.

The illegitimacy of authority weakens its effectiveness—just as weakness or ineffectiveness reduces belief in its legitimacy. The ineffectiveness and illegitimacy of authority have a solvent effect on the more inclusive collective self-conciousness of the various sectors of the pluralistic society. The process strengthens the individual self-consciousness of many individuals but it does not "atomize" society into an aggregate of separate self-interested individuals. It does produce a tendency in that direction but only to a limited extent. The chief immediate beneficiaries of the weakening of the collective self-consciousness of the society are the numerous particular sectors of the society. Their particular collective self-consciousnesses are fortified by the weakening of the collective self-consciousness of the entire society. The collective self-consciousness of the entire society is, in any case, never completely ascendant in the constituent sectors of society. It is always mixed with the respective particular collective self-consciousness of those sectors. No society can ever be a completely civil society, concerned only about the common good.

Civil politics, in accordance with its concern for the common good of society as a whole, assumes a belief that there is such a thing as "society as a whole." Society is not the market, although it has a place for the market. It is also not a political market of different, distinct and disjunctive interests, competing and incompatible or conflicting with each other. Since the idea of the good of the whole cannot be rigorously determined, there are inevitably different conceptions at any one time regarding the substance of the good of society as a whole.

That some politically active persons act civilly, i.e., for the good of the whole, does not mean that they are entirely lacking in partisanship. It does, however, mean that they are less partisan than some of their fellow partisans and their opponents, and that they speak and act more frequently and more visibly for the good of the larger society. They appeal to the recessive or latent civility of their fellow partisans and opponents and they sometimes succeed in arousing it and thereby strengthening it.

If the life of a liberal democratic society is to be peaceful enough and orderly enough to allow its citizens to go about their various businesses, the different sectors must be in a peaceful equilibrium with each other. It is not possible for this balance or equilibrium to be achieved or maintained only by rational bargaining in the market and by explicit rational compromise in political institutions. Differences of interest can usually be bargained over and fixed by contract, within the setting of a civil society. Differences of ideas usually cannot be reconciled, harmonized and made universally acceptable by a rational application of a clear criterion of the common good.

Of course, it would be very good if this could be done, but it is not likely. The belief that this is possible is one of the shortcomings of one popular current of contemporary academic social science. It is a worthy ideal but it is not realizable. It assumes a fundamental common interest which is inherent in society and which, once disclosed, will supervene over all other interests of the respective parties; it assumes rigorously persuasive rationality and relevant empirical knowledge of a high degree of precision and reliability. There are assumptions that evaluations can be very exactly formulated and compared with each other. If these modes of settling disagreement by contract and ratiocination cannot be practiced, the only alternative to disintegrative and rancorous conflict is some transparochial solidarity which is capable of holding the disagreements in check so that they do not become excessively wide or acute. I know that this is a bit like saying that the best way to overcome illness is to be well. I think that there is more to it than that.

IV

In which sections of the population can civility, rudimentary or highly developed, be found? Let me begin with the institutions and the professional custodians of those institutions which have in the past been regarded as the witnesses to transcendental values and as superior to partisanship. At first thought the universities might appear to be the most likely institutions of civil society. The universities should, in principle, be as disinterested among the contending interests and ideals as devotion to truth permits. The teachers in the universities should offer to society an authority standing outside the political struggle. They have performed these functions rather poorly in recent years.

Generally, universities as corporate bodies and their higher administrators have usually been neutral on public issues other than the scale of financial support by government. Universities as corporate bodies usually do not make declarations of their attitudes and recommendations regarding actions taken or to be taken by governments. This is far from true of individual university teachers, particularly in certain fields of study and especially so lately. Large numbers of them espouse one or another partisan attitude and, in the United States at least, the frequency with which they have attempted to persuade university administrators and sometimes the higher governing bodies of their universities to espouse a partisan policy has increased over the past few decades. University teachers are often partisans on behalf of their own pecuniary interests but they are no less often public partisans on behalf of the demands and what they regard as the interests of other parochial groups. In their teaching within the university, some of them espouse incivility and deny the existence of civil society.

The idiom and substance of the teaching of literature nowadays have in many Western universities become uncivilly partisan. Many teachers now assert that "oppression" is inherent in language and in works of literature. The teaching of literature has in many universities become politically partisan and inimical to civility. The hostility of teachers of humanities in the United States toward "the canon" is justified on ideological grounds. The teaching of sociology has been affected. In political science and anthropology, the "unmasking of oppression," "demythologization," the analysis of the "construction of tradition," etc., are less intellectual activities than they are political activities. They do not contribute to the order of civil society.

Nor is a great deal of help to be expected from the churches. Churches as such belong to the boundary between the earthly and transcendental realms. They are not in themselves parts of civil society; their society is the sacral society. But they also exist in the earthly realm of society, and in that role, they are or can be parts of civil society, although much of their history has been passed in societies which have not been civil societies.

The churches in Western societies have traditionally preached a single religion for all sectors of society; their deity was the deity of the entire society and of all mankind. Whereas the churches once behaved uncivilly in their espousal of the interests of the royal house and the aristocracy and great landowners and later of the class of wealthy private businessmen against the rest of the society—there were always some exceptions of clergymen who spoke on behalf of the entire society—now the churches, especially the more prominent clergymen of the major Protestant churches, share the political and social views of the more or less antinomian secular intellectuals. Similar attitudes are spreading among Roman Catholic intellectuals and priests. The sects and denominations disparaged as "fundamentalists" by the intellectuals of the major churches, sects and denominations are also in an aggrieved and resentful state of mind. Many of their members are patriots, but they seem to be unbridgeably separated from those whom they think of as ravaged by secularist views about many very important matters. An uncivil strife is rampant among the churches and sects; this strife is aggravated by the partisanship of more or less secularist collectivistic liberals, with an infusion of radicalism and of anguished, very conservative believers. None of the antagonists contributes to civility in the earthly religious sphere or in the political sphere.

At one time, the upper classes, inheritors of great wealth, the landowning aristocracy, prosperous merchants and industrialists produced a small number of public-spirited men and women who devoted much of their energy and some of their wealth to the protection of the common good; they also produced passive as well as vigorous exponents of a harsh incivility. One of the most striking features of the life of the liberal democracies of the past half century is the abdication from the civil roles which were once played by a significant handful of members of these strata. To some extent, this may be attributed to the loss of self-confidence which has afflicted the older upper classes in the face of egalitarian propaganda; perhaps they think that there is so much egalitarian prejudice against them that any efforts they make in public life would be certain to fail.

The new wealthy class, frequently rich by financial rather than industrial activities, has not offered much to compensate for the withdrawal of the stratum of the hereditarily wealthy and older plutocracy. The mass of the new wealthy class presents a spectacle of unrelenting pursuit of wealth and—unlike their earlier puritanical predecessors—great pleasure in spending it. Some of them go into politics and it is among these that some traces of civility are to be observed. Some of them engage in philanthropic activities; this too contributes to civil society.

The trade union movement, now that it has lost its socialist and communist *élan*, might be regarded as an alternative candidate to support civility. "Bread and butter" unionism has the civil merit of not being ideological. Yet the unyielding espousal of certain trade union demands in the decades following World War II has brought British and American industry into hazard. Lately they have shown a modest degree of conciliatoriness in industry.

The industrial working class which once had a marked sense of its own peripherality has in most liberal democratic countries come to regard itself as less remote from the center. Except for a small xenophobic and revolutionary margin, it has usually been moderately civil in the past half century in its relations with the center and with other peripheral groups. It is generally patriotic and in national crises even very patriotic. Although concerned with parochial benefits for itself, it has usually not shared in the extremes of doctrinaire class consciousness. It is probably even now the most civil of the major blocks of the population of present-day liberal democracies.

The intermittently uncivil attitude which was once present—not always salient—in the trade unions of the industrial working classes has lately been taken over by trade unions of white-collar workers, e.g., civil servants, postal workers, airport controllers, nurses and physicians and even university teachers. In most cases, their incivility is usually not ideological but it is uncivil nonetheless. Some of these occupations and professions were once markedly civil in the sense in which we have been using the term here.

The rural and small-town population was often civil within its own restricted radius. It was usually patriotic. The rural population has dwindled very much in its numerical position in present-day liberal democratic societies and it has also lost much of its high moral status. It is moreover very concerned to exploit what advantages still accrue to it from the mercantilist governmental tradition of being nationally self-sufficient in the production of food. In situations of damaged economic fortunes, the rural population has increased in incivility, but generally these conditions are not the normal ones.

In a different sector of the population the prevailing pattern of conduct is almost wholly uncivil in its disruptive intrusions into domestic and economic private life. I speak of the rather large unemployed *lumpenproletariat* and the criminal and delinquent class in the United States. All large urban societies have had *lumpenproletariats*. Prolonged unemployment has added to their numbers so that there are many young persons in certain parts of the urban population in the United States and Great Britain who grow up without the expectation of earning their own livelihood by continuous work. Prominent in the criminal and delinquent classes in the United States are adolescents, largely black but by no means entirely so, who ravage whole areas of the large cities to an extent which makes their depredations statistically normal features of urban life. This incivility is not only to be found in the *lumpenproletariat*. It is also found among fully and regularly employed young persons who find the routines of daily life too boring or too frustrating. Their activities have become statistically normal and morally abnormal to such an extent that they have to be reckoned with in the daily life of the residents of large cities. There has come to be a breakdown of the civil order far beyond the powers of the police to confine and reduce it. This does not prevent the routines of life from being carried on but it requires adaptations which are constrictions to civil order of law abidingness which protects the domestic sphere. This phenomenon is not confined to the United States.

The routine crimes of the criminal and delinquent class on the scale on which they are carried out are indeed not only in themselves severe infringements on the order ostensibly guaranteed by law but there have from time to time been more extreme manifestations in riots which are gross infringements on the order of civil society.

The widespread consumption of narcotics which is characteristic of the young generation of criminals or delinquents is not confined to that generation. It is by now an enduring practice of a generation of mature years, whose immersion in the economy and culture of the consumption of narcotics brings them very close to the recurrent commission of criminal actions. There are many young and not so young persons who consume narcotics but who are not otherwise criminals; this may be true particularly of the consumers of "soft drugs."

The consumption of narcotics as well as the practice of homosexuality are nowadays regarded by many persons as belonging in the private sphere and enjoying the prerogatives of private liberty.

In fact, they are not confined to the private sphere; they encroach into the public or civil sphere and aggravate the situation. The consumption of narcotics is linked with large-scale criminal activities which are also major economic enterprises with long-standing and highly organized criminal traditions.

Criminals and addicts to narcotics are nothing new in large urbanized societies. All large cities have had a large *lumpenproletariat*, large enough to cause much civil disorder. I need only cite the Gordon Riots in London in 1780 or the riots in St. Louis and Chicago in 1919 or the riots in the ghettos of New York, Los Angeles, and other American cities in the 1960s to indicate that the *lumpenproletariat* in a state of excitation is capable of disrupting and overpowering civil society, even if only transiently and locally. It is reasonable to think that the "successes" of the rioters, i.e., the avoidance of severe repression, have reduced the legitimacy of the indulgent and weak authority and encouraged further incivility. Where the authority is strong enough in will and force to put down these severe disruptions of the reign of legal order, its action often entails "states of emergency" curfews, acts which cripple, at least for a time, the institutions of civil society.

V

No society is a shining model of civil society. A society which would be entirely civil is difficult to imagine, but if one does succeed in forming some notion of what it would be like, it appears to be undesirable. A society in which no one thought of anything but the common good might be extremely boring, spiritually impoverished and intellectually infertile. Disagreement, individual self-seeking initiatives, saying things which might give offense, breaking away from the cover of the collective self-consciousness, are part of the spice of life. But there can be too much of a good thing. That is where civility has its proper place as a restraining power in the public sphere.

The situation of civility in liberal democratic societies is not wholly gratifying to persons who care about the survival and effectiveness of those societies. There are open breaches. There are large blocks of incivility at the peripheries with which the agents of the centers cannot cope. There are recurrent outbursts of incivility in the centers. Yet these societies remain liberal democratic; the institutions of civil society continue to function. They do endure and even, from time to time, improve; some of the improvements are long-lasting. In view of the challenges to civility created by the pluralistic, liberal democratic nature of these societies, the achievement seems to be unique in world history. The institutions of civil society are sustained not only by civility but also by rational reflection on the benefits they confer on the pursuit of interests. But it is the ingredient of civility which makes the difference between their survival and their decay.

TWO

CIVIC VIRTUE

INTERESTED AND DISINTERESTED CITIZENS

Katherine Auspitz

> I doubt whether men were better in aristocratic times, though certainly they talked incessantly about the beauties of virtue. Only in secret did they study its utility.
>
> Alexis de Tocqueville, *Democracy in America*[1]

Civic virtue, I think, should not be praised and lamented as a lost form of selflessness. Good citizens will act from both interested and disinterested motives; and encounters with fellow-citizens, recognized as moral equals, will discipline their self-assertion. Liberty itself, reliably and uniquely, fosters enlightened self-interest and an understanding of the interests of others.

I will argue that the Renaissance ideal of civic virtue was enlarged, during the eighteenth and nineteenth centuries, to include conduct of which most citizens might be imagined capable. Free government, its advocates believed, demanded from all citizens both thought and passion; thus it necessarily confronted them with the power and obduracy of opposing convictions and commitments. Resignation, or mutual respect, taught moderation. The experience of citizenship itself made individuals, at once, better able to discern their own and the public interest.

I acknowledge that historians too often conjure up such "traditions" as suit their polemical purpose; they make philosophers, posthumously and with no recourse, precursors of movements that would have horrified them. Nonetheless, I think the project I describe—setting out the moral and social bases of self-government—has been understood by those who advanced it over the centuries as a common and continuing effort.

To summarize historically: Machiavelli celebrated *virtù* during the Renaissance as a rare and heroic, but yet attainable, classical ideal. Later, in the Enlightenment, philosophers expected civic virtue to arise as the predictable, though not the inevitable or unintended, consequence of living in a properly constituted state. Finally, in the nineteenth century, democrats and prudent conservatives came to regard civic virtue not only as a worthy goal, but as an urgent practical necessity. I believe it to be an urgent practical necessity still.

To summarize conceptually: In each of these periods, writers supported their exhortations to civic virtue with a professedly realist political analysis which agreed on these three points:

1. that self-mastery was a worthier and also a more feasible ideal than self-denial;

2. that the sense of self appropriate to citizens can develop only among equals;

3. that equality need not be absolute; rather, some social differentiation is inevitable and can itself help preserve liberty.

I begin with the civic humanism of the Renaissance and with Machiavelli's *virtù*, which is, notably, neither a Christian nor a cloistered virtue. This starting place is very much *in medias res*. One can scarcely speak of politics, or of social animals, or of virtue without invoking Aristotle; and patristic writing was grounded in classical, especially Aristotelean, philosophy. The contemporary German Thomist Josef Pieper, for example, emphasizes that Thomas Aquinas understood the four cardinal virtues, prudence, justice, fortitude, and temperance, to be "perfected abilities" and human nature realized not denied by their practice.[2] *Ratio*, reason, was honored very much in the observance by the Scholastics; and knights vigorously prosecuted wars they deemed to be just, rarely turning the other cheek. But I am not concerned to assess the degrees of continuity and discontinuity between medieval and Renaissance thought.

Machiavelli plainly describes a new moral sphere: paradise, perhaps, cannot be regained, but the *polis* might be. The City of Man seems no longer an antechamber for the world to come but the world itself, a heady, dangerous, thrilling place. Machiavelli brings virtue back to its Latin root, *vir*, connoting manliness or prowess, meanings that had not been conspicuous in its pious uses. *Virtù* enables man to take events into his own hands and shape them according to his will. He counters the flux, the wildness, and frenzy of fortune with his own steady nerve, purpose, and insight. Of the cardinal virtues, prudence and courage remain, fused in the new.[3] There is a combative energy about a virtuous act; and the act, to exhibit *virtù* in this sense, must effect a desired end.

Machiavelli himself purports always to speak of "the effectual truth of the thing, rather than the imagination of it." Prudence is essential; unthinking goodness, dangerous:

> For a man who wants to make a profession of good in all regards must come to ruin among so many who are not good. Hence it is necessary...to learn to be able not to be good, and to use this and not use it according to necessity.[4]

This, I think, is not an impious notion. Providence manifestly permits unmerited suffering, and, thus, a man responsible for Florence must protect Florentines. He cannot blindly do justice whilst permitting the heavens to fall upon his fellow citizens. It is in this sense, I think, that the famous willingness to risk one's soul for Florence must be understood.

Above all, the virtuous deed must effect the desired end. And I would emphasize, as I think Machiavelli himself did, that bringing about the end is more important than justifying it. Mercy will sometimes be advisable, pitiless vengeance will serve on other occasions. Heedless, reckless *beaux gestes* and the self-indulgence of the *acte gratuite* are excluded also, no less impolitic, no less reprehensible than inopportune piety. But his most important message, an exhortation, is a heartening one, that men are capable of doing whatever needs to be done. The fabulous virtuosi of the past were not so different from us: "although these men were rare and marvelous, nonetheless they were also men."[5]

Machiavelli found more than inspiration in ancient history; he found, also, cautionary tales of civil strife and corruption. His

Discourses on the First Ten Books of Livy, like his more contemporary *Florentine Histories,* are about conflict, not so much with foreign enemies but among fellow citizens, conflict between haves and have-nots. Machiavelli would dismiss, for example, Hannah Arendt's notion that ancient republics were irrecoverably and self-lessly civic.

He speculates in *The Discourses* about the proper institutional context for virtue. He begins with a typology of constitutions like Aristotle's: three forms of government, rule by the one, the few or the many—three forms or six, for each regime is susceptible of corruption. A principality may decline into tyranny, the rule of worthy aristocrats (*ottimati*) into oligarchy, or popular government into anarchic license (*licenzioso*). He, like Aristotle, recommends mixed government, so that the good qualities of each element may stabilize the city.

But also, and this point is crucial for an understanding of free government: Machiavelli does not assume an identity of interest among citizens. He takes for granted that nobles and plebeians will pursue conflicting interests, but that these conflicts need not, necessarily, endanger the republic. Quite the reverse. "All legislation favorable to liberty is brought about by the clash between them."[6]

He assumes neither self-sacrifice nor *noblesse oblige.* The "haves" were, in his view, more likely than others to cause disturbances: not merely is greed insatiable but the flux of fortune creates among the rich fear that their wealth may diminish relative to another's. These anxieties incite them always to seek more, "for men are inclined to think that they cannot hold securely what they possess unless they get more at others' expense." The people will anticipate this and take measures to protect themselves. Nor, Machiavelli observes, "can a republic reasonably be stigmatized as in any way disordered in which there occur such striking examples of *virtù.*" He affirms that the demands of a free people are very seldom harmful to liberty, for they are due either to the reality of the people's being oppressed, or to the people's suspicion that it shortly will be.[7]

Moreover, sustained repression emasculates the city and unfits it for war. Rulers disregard the populace at their peril: if they intend ever to associate the citizenry in important undertakings, they must pay attention to it. (This caveat is linked with his vilification of mercenaries and his great regard for the morale of the citizen-soldier. "Good soldiers can always find gold, gold cannot always find good soldiers.")[8]

It is not social strife, but social inequality, with its inevitable consequence, personal power, that corrupts republics. Holdings need not be identical, but no citizen ought to dispose of the means to subjugate others:

> ...if a citizen is to do harm and is to obtain extraordinary authority, he must have many attributes which he ought not to be allowed to possess; he will need to be very rich and to have numerous adherents and partisans, which he cannot have so long as the laws are strictly observed.[9]

Machiavelli fears the patron-client relation: men rich enough to maintain a swarming clientele, courtiers or armed retainers who can be employed to subdue or corrupt private citizens. But proximate equality is not enough. The city must also afford outlets for "changeful humors" so that citizens will employ normal, that is acknowledged and legitimate means of redress. Denied lawful means, they will find subversive ones, recourse to foreign allies or to private forces. Thus, the citizens' primary allegiance to the city will be compromised, and factions harden into sects.[10]

He elaborates this point in the *Florentine Histories* in a passage that Rousseau will one day invoke to illustrate the relation between particular interests and the general will (cf. below, p. 30).

> ...those who hope a republic can be united are very much deceived in this hope...some divisions are harmful to republics and some are helpful. Those that are harmful are accompanied by sects and partisans; those that are helpful are maintained without sects or partisans. Thus, since a founder of a republic can not provide that there be no enmities in it, he has to provide at least that there be no sects.[11]

Divisions and factions there will inevitably be, but properly channeled they can strengthen not weaken the city. "Nothing does so much to stabilize a republic as some institution whereby the changeful humors which agitate it are afforded a proper outlet by way of law."[12] *Virtù* drives interest as well as fortune through the proper channels, as dikes and canals arrest and employ the torrential energy of the sea.

Montesquieu, whose *Considerations on the Grandeur of the Romans and their Decline* follows Machiavelli closely, agrees that the orderly state is not static: citizens simultaneously pursue their own and the general interest; and to wish people hardy in war, timid in peace, zealous in defending themselves against foreign oppressors and supine before domestic tyrants, Montesquieu cautions, is to wish the impossible. He states, as a general rule, that whenever a state that calls itself a republic appears tranquil, it cannot be free. Free political unions are polyphonic; and however opposed their parties may appear, they all contribute (*concourent*) to the general good of the society, "as dissonance in music contributes to the total accord."[13]

Montesquieu brings to the study of society arresting metaphors from Newtonian physics. In society, as in the universe, bodies are "eternally linked by the action of one, the reaction of others." Only in utter despotism is there real, that is fixed, division rather than dynamic and shifting equilibrium. In the absence of liberty, some men oppress others *without resistance:* this is not an achieved consensus, but the stillness of the grave, "...not the citizens united but their dead bodies entombed (*ensevelis*) side by side."[14] Montesquieu's Rome, like Machiavelli's, seethes with virtue and treachery.

But his typology of regimes, elaborated in the very important and original *Spirit of the Laws*, departs significantly from Machiavelli's: he abandons the rule of the one, the few, and the many, for a scheme at once more complete and more judgmental. He describes three kinds of government—republican, monarchical, and despotic—but only two types of society, equal and unequal, composed respectively of individuals and of groups of individuals. Further, a uniquely appropriate "spring" of action animates each political form. Virtue upholds the republic, and honors the kingdom; while despotism demands only fear. A fourth constitutional possibility, the aristocratic republic, depends on moderation which approaches virtue. His scheme is worth visualizing (see Figure 2-1).

The spring, *ressort*, is a watchmaker's term: *le ressort qui fait mouvoir*, the spring that makes it tick. Montesquieu takes great care to explain that one will encounter honor in republics and virtuous conduct in monarchies. (To say, he explains, that this wheel or that pin does not make the watch move is not to say it is missing from the mechanism altogether.) One may find them even among

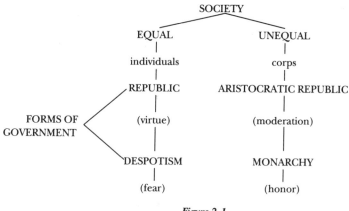

Figure 2-1

the subjects of a despot, although not in the tyrant himself, for he is a social isolate, and all virtue and all honor must be exercised among peers. Montesquieu grants that "the force of the law and the arm of the prince," that is, the momentum of established power, will keep most governments running. But not republics. Republics require an additional impetus, *un ressort de plus*, civic virtue.

And this virtue he calls a simple thing, a "very simple thing, it's love of the republic; a feeling, not a conclusion" (*"un sentiment et pas une suite des connaissances"*).[15] The feeling manifests itself, not in collective frenzies of self-sacrifice, but in a sustained and deliberate preference for the public good. To be a virtuous citizen of a republic, whatever else one does, one must be ever mindful of the public consequences of one's actions.

He further recognized civic virtue as love of equality, both the structural equality that prevents divisions from freezing into permanent superiority and subordination, and the psychological equality that permits one citizen to enter imaginatively into the thoughts of another.

For this reason, republican government requires all the powers of education to promote suitable mores. Simplicity and frugality are essential because devotion to the common cause becomes more likely, Montesquieu suggests, when private appetites are denied satisfaction. Honor in a monarchy, on the other hand, demands a less exigent education, more can be left to nature: honor is "encouraged (*favorisé*) by the passions and encourages them in its turn."[16] Virtue is always somewhat painful, rare, and ephemeral; and he seems to anticipate the archetypical Jacobin, *pur et dur*. Ever devoted to the golden mean, Montesquieu admits there can be too much of a good thing, even virtue.

Montesquieu's sociology makes the fragility of republican virtue particularly ominous because the inescapable alternative, for egalitarian societies, is despotism. Both republican and despotic governments presuppose social equality: individuals, free-standing, capable of association, but not compulsorily or "naturally," that is ascriptively, affiliated.

What then are the prospects for civic life in those regimes, monarchies and aristocratic republics whose citizens are not so equal? In both these forms, social groupings, "intermediary bodies," prevent individuals from experiencing their citizenship in an unmediated way; and, therefore, citizens are not expected to identify their private interests so closely with the public good. Montesquieu suggests that "honor, that is to say, the prejudice of each person and each station (*condition*) takes the place of political virtue and represents it everywhere."[17]

Honor rests upon invidious distinctions and serves to maintain and emphasize social differences. By scrupulous attention to *punctilio*, by insistence upon prerogative, social bodies restrain the sovereign. *Esprit de corps* permits intermediary bodies acting collectively and their members acting individually to promote the common good obliquely. Bodies are held in orbit by a balance of centrifugal and centripetal forces (*une force qui éloigne sans cesse du centre tous les corps, et une force de pesanteur qui les y ramène*). Montesquieu, ever delicate, refrains from suggesting that the Sun King, had he better understood the nature of things, might have permitted his satellites a more independent course. But he is emphatic: *Point de noblesse, point de monarche, point de monarche, point de noblesse*. Without moral and constitutional peers, a ruler becomes something other than a king.[18]

Honor forbids base deeds and inspires noble ones (*belles actions*); Montesquieu gives two appealing examples: Crillon refusing to assassinate the duc de Guise but offering to fight him; and the vicomte d'Ortho declining to participate in the St. Bartholomew's Day massacre, "...we implore Your Majesty to employ our arms and our lives in *choses faisables*, in things that can be done."[19]

Some things are simply not done: slaughtering civilians, for example. Montesquieu understands that such glorious insubordination is as likely to arise from vanity and *amour-propre* as from pity or toleration. But no matter. Self-respect serves social ends, and self-respect can be found by distancing oneself from one's fellows, as well as by drawing near to them.

A delicate balance of distinction and rapport, private interest and public spirit, also supports that curiously mixed form, the aristocratic republic. I would suggest careful attention to this form, for, I believe, it will serve also to describe a very contemporary hope, a pluralist republic, a republic in which the freedom to associate assumes great importance. Moderation, Montesquieu thinks, acts as the soul (*âme*) of the aristocratic republic; and it is significant that this *juste-milieu* polity, like a fine character, is prompted to action by a soul, rather than set in motion like a machine. Moderation here recalls temperance, the last named and least heroic of the cardinal virtues.

Montesquieu held that republican motivation must be, by definition, well-intended; and, indeed, the moderation exercised by citizens of an aristocratic or pluralist republic, powerful notables or powerful interest groups, must be a most commendable self-mastery: restraint in the interest of comity. It ought never to be confused with an indifference to the common good arising from cowardice or sloth (*lâcheté, paresse*). Instead, moderation must be understood as a form of magnanimity: the winners do not press their advantage. They do not humiliate and estrange the losers; they agree to disagree and keep talking.

Aristocratic republics, especially commercial ones, Montesquieu thought might tolerate considerable differences in fortune. Two sorts of inequality, however, he judges subversive of them: First, extreme inequality between the governed and the governors will destroy that minimal likeness republics must preserve among their citizens. Differences in fortune, however, are not so dangerous in themselves as legal or fiscal privilege. Equality before the law is a *sine qua non* of a republic. Second, any inequality among members of the various intermediary bodies threatens their internal solidarity and prevents them from acting as they must to preserve the constitutional balance of power.

Honor and moderation both depend upon *esprit de corps* and *amour-propre*; and, in his discussion of aristocratic motives, Montesquieu seems to rely upon the analysis of self-love and self-interest developed a century before by moralists like La Rochefoucauld. La Rochefoucauld's *Maximes* dismiss both virtue— "virtue never goes so far as when vanity accompanies it"—and moderation—an attempt to "appear greater than one's fortune"— and he introduces his *aperçus* with the thought that "...it is not always through valor and chastity that men are valiant and women are chaste."[20]

The witty duke has been charged with contributing to the "demolition of the hero."[21] However, some eighteenth century liberals, I think particularly of the Scottish Enlightenment, found his insights distinctly encouraging. Admirable behavior need not stem from praiseworthy motives—well then, if virtue, valor, honor, and constancy arise from interest and vanity, they are well within everyone's reach. La Rochefoucauld had written:

> *Amour-propre* is love of one's self and of all things for the self: it makes men idolaters of themselves and tyrants over others if fortune gives them the means...[22]

But he continued "its transformations surpass those of metamorphosis, its refinements those of chemistry." Further, self-love is so protean, so fugitive that it can only catch glimpses of itself in the eyes of others. Adam Smith made crisp sense of this psychology: if all things are vanity, he concluded, then "the great secret of education is to direct vanity toward its proper objects."[23] Radical selfishness is frightening only if one despairs of shaping the right sort of self.

Smith's text engages La Rochefoucauld closely. The duke had analyzed friendship in economic terms:

> Maxim LXXXIII. "What men call friendship is only a society, only a reciprocal managing of interests, an exchange of good offices; it's nothing, finally, but a commerce in which self-love seeks always something to gain."[24]

Smith reaches a different conclusion about exchange itself in *The Theory of Moral Sentiments*: although society could exist "among different men as among different merchants, from a sense of its utility...a mercenary exchange of good offices,"[25] it does not, as a matter of actual fact, work that way.

It is curious that nineteenth century counter-revolutionary writ-ers taxed the Enlightenment with naiveté. I think the major minds in Paris and in Edinburgh were singularly free from delusions about human perfectibility or social utopias. All agreed altruism could not be relied upon; and some preferred to dispense with it altogether, positing only rationally self-interested individuals. Sir James Steuart, for example, wrote in his *Inquiry into the Principles of Political Economy* that

> ...were a people to become quite disinterested, there would be no possibility of governing them. Everyone might consider the interests of his own country in a different light, and may join in the ruin of it, by endeavoring to pro-mote its advantage.[26]

Sir James judged "public spirit" to be fully as superfluous (and presumably also as rare) in a well-governed state as "miracles are in a religion once fully established," and yet he professed to esteem and admire "every act of public spirit, every sentiment of disinter-estedness" achieved by persons living under "ill-administered governments,"[27] regimes perhaps not so rare. Other thinkers, Rousseau and Adam Smith, among them, maintained that any sta-ble political allegiance must rest upon a recognized convergence of private and public interest, but also to some degree upon disin-terested commitment and upon feelings for one's fellow citizens.

Moreover, they were convinced that these necessary feelings were prior to reason, or at any rate, coequal with it. Rousseau posi-tively asserts two principles prior to reason, self-love (*amour-de-soi*), which tends to self-preservation, and a second which inspires in us a natural repugnance at seeing another person suffer and which tends to the preservation of the species. Smith insists that we share other people's pleasure and pain "so instantaneously, and often upon such frivolous occasions"[28] that our response cannot possibly arise from self-interested calculations about reciprocity.

David Hume concurs, "the interests of society are not, even on their own account, entirely indifferent to us." Fellow feeling is "experienced to be a principle in human nature."[29] Note that they do not say we should experience vicarious sorrow and joy, but that we do.

Rousseau notes two aspects of this process: first, the naturalness of compassion, the original social virtue, and the source of all the others. Next, that commiseration is more energetic the more intimately the "spectator animal" identifies with the "suffering animal."[30] How then do animals identify?

Society, once created, presents them with *semblables*, and together they engender social selves. The savage, Rousseau wrote in the *Discourse on the Origins of Inequality*, "lives within himself, the social man is always outside himself (*hors de lui*)," fashioned by laws and mores. Adam Smith, too, saw man as a spectator, taught civility by his observations. Society might exist merely as a commerce, but inevitably it serves also as a "mirror." We learn about ourselves from the ways in which others react to us: we are, willy-nilly, civilized by these encounters. But "our senses never did and never can carry us beyond our own person...it is by imagination only that we can form any conception of what others themselves sense."[31] Spectators, we must be; impartial spectators we can become through social intercourse that cultivates an imaginative understanding of other people.

Conversation, Smith believed, "restores the mind to tranquillity because the sympathy we seek can only be achieved by presenting our joys and sorrows in such a way that others can enter into them."[32] We put things in perspective, we appeal to common bonds; Smith clearly thought confidences would be constrained by decorum and propriety, and one could as plausibly expect that people will rage and weep, magnifying their troubles to gain sympathy. Nonetheless, I think it is true that giving an account, almost any intelligible account of an experience, prevents excessive self-absorption. Conversation, thus understood, becomes a metaphor for politics: citizens represent themselves in ways their fellow citizens will understand.

Intersubjectivity is at the core of this public identity, as is self-respect. Rousseau wrote: "Respect your fellow citizens and you will make yourself respectable." Smith goes farther and makes self-esteem a prerequisite of virtuous action. "No action can properly be called virtuous which is not accompanied with the sentiment of self-approbation."[33]

In his *Inquiry into the Origins of Honor*, Bernard Mandeville, better known for *The Fable of the Bees* and its proposition that private vices can, by "dexterous Management," be turned into public benefits, presents a subtle view of the social *persona*. With his usual studied audacity, he suggests that sensible rulers not merely encourage self-approbation, but strive to make man "an Object of

Reverence to himself." And, indeed, the signers of the American Declaration of Independence pledged their "sacred honor."

Mandeville's *Inquiry* takes the form of a dialogue: the skeptical questioner imagines that a man might esteem and love himself, but how is it possible to hold oneself in awe? Cleomenes, the author's voice, explains we are afraid of the "Notion we form of the opinion of others." And that honorable self-image once internalized offers many advantages. Self-scrutiny cannot be evaded, "...in worshipping Honor, a Man adores himself which is ever dear to him, never absent."

> Innumerable Sins are committed in private which the Presence of a Child, or the most insignificant Person might have hindered, by Men who believe God to be omniscient and never questioned his Ubiquity.[34]

The rewards of honor, unlike those of self-denying virtue, are "ravishing," and they appeal to the "Instinct of Sovereignty" which Mandeville deems natural to man. More important, honor preserves certain inclinations necessary to the state. He gives as an example the efforts by the marshals of France to regulate but not abolish duelling: "they lay no more restraint on the Spirit of Revenge, than Matrimony does on the Desire of Procreation."[35] Moral codes must be realistic and preserve useful energies, the necessary modicum of restraint cultivated by art, custom and education.

The urbane Mandeville upholds the realism of the liberal tradition. What then of the republicans' hardest case, Rousseau and the supposedly mystical general will? The infamous forcing to be free? I think the political self presented in the *Social Contract* is a whole and plausible one, at once interested and disinterested, able to pursue private as well as common ends. That self is not, as Hannah Arendt would have it, a tormented *âme déchirée*. That phrase does not even appear in the *Social Contract*; Miss Arendt, whose misunderstanding of civic virtue I will discuss, along with some others, in conclusion, imports that tortured member, uncited, from the more self-pitying autobiographical works.[36]

Rousseau's pre-contractual beings advance rather than abandon self-interest in agreeing to unite. Some interests are common, others are not. If individual interests were identical, he remarks, politics would cease to be an art, and there would be no need to fashion a general will. Rousseau aspires to connect "that which right permits with what interest prescribes." He imagines the total surrender of each to all as a way to avoid partial and personal sub-ordination.[37]

This speaks to Machiavelli's mistrust—and indeed to the persistent practical problem—of personal power exerted through entourages and clienteles. Rousseau noted Machiavelli's strictures about sectarian politics in his notes to the 1762 edition of the *Social Contract*;[38] and, like Machiavelli, he feared not division among citizens, but partial associations that would interfere with the expression of individual differences. Factions create fewer, not more, divisions among citizens, and thus make political debate less general. He feared even more the creation of a single, a unique, polarizing difference. If there must be partial associations within the state, he recommended, let there be many: a sentiment echoed by modern political scientists who speak of "cross-cutting cleavages." Above all, let citizens enter into them as equals. Republican associations must differ radically from the asymmetrical bonds of fealty.

Towards the end of the eighteenth century, it did appear that some of the older forms of domination were losing control. Money had been a great solvent. Adam Smith took evident joy in recording that merchants had delivered the inhabitants of the countryside from "servile dependency upon their superiors." A market economy created reciprocal ties among people who had previously exchanged goods and services on the basis of custom, deference, or extortion. Alexis de Tocqueville, free of nostalgia for feudalism, acknowledged the savagery of a time when "men had only one means of acting upon one another, force."[39] In modern times, intelligence as well as wealth afforded other means. A *de facto* social pluralism had come about, multiplying the sources of power and influence, creating perhaps the sort of differentiation that might protect liberty and encourage moderation. Enthusiasts of republican virtue thought its time might be coming,

Nonetheless, attention to the market and to the act of exchange did not obscure another, more troubling, economic activity, production. Adam Smith, who had nothing but praise for the division of labor *a propos* of the manufacture of pins, warned that work which affords a man "no occasion to exert his understanding" will make him "as stupid and as ignorant as it is possible for a human creature to become." These fears gave an urgency, a preemptive or precautionary character to arguments for civic virtue. Smith urged that governments take "proper pains" to promote military exercises and encourage, or if necessary compel, primary education, to preserve the populace from the "mutilation and wretchedness" which repetitive, mechanical tasks would otherwise inflict.[40]

Throughout the nineteenth century, it would be argued that politics provides a sphere for the "exercise of faculties that work neither engages nor develops...preserving many energetic natures from demoralization.[41] And as revolutions became more frequent, the urgent necessity of civic virtue became more apparent. One of the three French workers elected to the National Assembly in 1848 would defend the people's "great and legitimate need for a public life," and also threaten that, denied a "broad intellectual participation in the general movement of things, (the people) will squander its generous sap." He conjures the bloody—and onanistic— futility of tumults that do not bear institutional fruit.[42]

Tocqueville saw in the events of 1848 an "obscure and erroneous notion of right which, joined with a brutal force, communicates to it an energy, a tenacity, a power which it would not have alone."[43] Nonetheless, a concern for right preserved moral discourse, and rights once enjoyed, *droits acquis*, gave a stake in the system, akin to property but, unlike property, infinitely extensible. Political participation was expected to counteract the damaging effects of the industrial division of labor and to encourage moderation. Citizens had a lot more to lose than their chains.

Democrats and prudent conservatives undertook to educate egoism; increasingly, they came to believe that people could not identify their own interests properly—could not achieve enlightened self-interest—without the exercise of civil rights and civil liberties: the franchise, freedom of speech, press, assembly, and association. And it was exercise precisely that they prescribed: human faculties, natural but latent, could be cultivated by citizenship as by no other social activity. Politics was seen as the great conversation through which people learn to represent themselves properly. All men and women need not be heroically, selflessly virtuous—few heroes were that; indeed, they could legitimately continue to pursue private ends. But so long as persons pursued their ends peacefully and openly, through liberties they accorded all others, they would become other than merely self-regarding.

J.S. Mill and Tocqueville himself are the most familiar champions of this point of view; but all over western Europe, the same arguments were advanced by entrepreneurs and autodidact artisans, by picaresque counts fighting for the *Risorgimento*, by tailors organizing cooperative groceries in the East Era of London, by free-thinkers' circulating libraries in Burgundy, by striking workers in the Rhineland, by myriads of district visiting ladies and school teachers. If there was ever *Zeitgeist* this was it. It is impossible to over-estimate their earnestness: educate and uplift, *instruire et moraliser, Volksbildung ist Volksbefreiung.*

Tocqueville's *Democracy in America* presents the most ramified account of the ways in which enlightened self-interest might support free institutions in an egalitarian society, a state to which he believed all nations were progressing. He feared that materialism would corrupt the "springs of action" and interest, narrowly reckoned, replace warmer feelings. Yet he found Americans making good use of self-interest properly understood

> ...by itself it (self-interest) cannot make a man virtuous, but its discipline shapes a lot of orderly, temperate, moderate, careful, and self-controlled citizens. If it does not lead the will directly to virtue, it establishes habits which unconsciously turn it that way.[44]

Though it is a truism that individuals will advance their own interests, he said, it remains to be seen what they will believe those interests to be. Like the eighteenth century writers he diligently studied (and he is supposed to have travelled with volumes of Montesquieu and Rousseau), Tocqueville assumed social identity to be malleable. He distinguished, pointedly, between egoism, which is depraved and "springs from blind instinct," and individualism, which is misguided, mistaken, "due more to inadequate understanding than to perversity of the heart."

Happily, liberty remedies both the error and the vice. Voluntary associations and decentralized power serve, as Montesquieu expected intermediary bodies would, to restrain sovereign power. But for Tocqueville they do more, they educate and ennoble: "the heart is enlarged and the mind is enlightened by the reciprocal influence of man upon man."[45]

J. S. Mill cherished the same hopes—specifically with regard to two categories of persons whose supposedly ungovernable appetites educated men found threatening and often incomprehensible, workers and women. What do they want? Perhaps, Mill suggests, we should ask them. Writing in 1861, with most laborers still excluded from the franchise in Britain, Mill has a nice sense of the limits of vicarious sympathy. "How different and how infinitely less superficial" parliamentary debate on social questions would be if workers were represented in the House of Commons. Who among its members, he asks, can "ever for an instant look at any question with the eyes of a working man"?[46]

Mill takes the position that not only has the worker the right to be represented and, indeed, the duty to develop his rational and affective faculties in public life, but in addition, his participation will educate others by confronting them with experiences hitherto inaccessible to them. Thus all citizens become more complete, debate more inclusive, policy wiser. Mill's feminism develops the same themes: there can be neither love nor loyalty among strangers: "...thorough knowledge of one another hardly ever exists, but between persons who, besides being intimates, are equals."[47]

It is not, however, wise policy that he principally seeks; more important for Mill than any particular outcome is the human development accomplished in the process. He expresses his most damning criticism of despotism with a rhetorical question: "What sort of person can be formed under such a system?" Treacherous persons, resentful persons, incendiary persons, craven and snivelling persons. Nineteenth century democrats believed liberty alone made the right sort of person.

Mill does not argue, for example, that jury trial is the best way to ascertain the truth of conflicting claims; he is, however, positively convinced the jurors will be better people for having served, for their exposure to due process, and for the thought-experiment in impartiality they will have shared.

Similarly, he argues in *On Liberty* that many things which might be better done by the state, by competent functionaries, should be left to individuals or private associations because it is better that individuals attempt them. They will benefit more from trying and failing than from any advantage passively enjoyed. "Action is the food of feeling," he says, and if an individual can do nothing to help his fellows or his community, he will feel little for them.

Tocqueville, full of loathing for the Second Empire, wrote in a similar vein, that the simulacrum of liberty will not suffice. If a citizen senses that his participation is meaningless, he will withhold it. "The affections of man turn toward power"; and democracy can not work as a plebiscitory figleaf on a bureaucratic colossus.

Democratic politics is partly expressive and partly instrumental. Civic virtue depends upon self-respect grounded in a sense of justice, but also in a sense of efficacy. I want to speculate a bit about the continuing relevance of these notions, but before I do that, I want to dispense with some contemporary approaches to virtue that strike me as ill-conceived.

Hannah Arendt, whose exaltation of republican virtue in *On Revolution* is matched only by her contempt for the poor, presents a curiously bloodless picture of classical politics. Machiavelli and Montesquieu analyzed the perpetual strife between rich and poor in Rome, Machiavelli concluding, "Good laws arise from tumults." Miss Arendt would have politics so disinterested as to be devoid of substance; her citizens are poseurs, gesticulating in the forum, burdened by nothing so demeaning as a program. It is unclear what, apart from questions of constitutional law, would be discussed in the "public spaces" wherein questions of poverty and want ought never to intrude. Dismissing the poor as enslaved to the "needs of their bodies," she obscures a point Rousseau well understood. In society, bonds of servitude exist between persons. Begging, or prostitution, or slavery degrades, hunger does not. Deprivation, bodily or psychic, can prompt a variety of responses, some of them virtuous. Hannah Arendt exemplifies one sort of romantic disdain for interested politics, a pseudo-classical refusal to grant that the struggles of "civil society" are the stuff of politics.[48]

Alasdair MacIntyre's *After Virtue* displays an altogether different nostalgia, for a time when ethical or political questions could be settled: he laments "a disquieting private arbitrariness" and the interminable clash of "conceptually incommensurable" imperatives. He acknowledges the worth of the republican tradition, civic virtue as "those dispositions that uphold that overriding allegiance (to a public good)." But, he ignores the complexity of the history he evokes. When were competing moral claims not "incommensurable"? Did a stoic and an epicurean reach agreement more easily than a social democrat and a libertarian? He, like many communitarians, hates the static of liberty, the dissidence of dissent. Yet his closing vision, the shades of Trotsky and St. Benedict hovering over a more loving humankind, seems to me to offer some conceptual incommensurabilities all its own.[49]

I differ, too, with those who despair of the future of free institutions because they believe them to be based on some "pre-liberal" or "pre-modern" and dwindling religious capital. Both capitalism and democracy, some say, require discipline which they cannot themselves engender. This notion equates virtue with self-denial; the republican conception of virtue as disciplined self-assertion, I believe to be at once more encouraging and more realistic. *Virtù*, as Machiavelli understood it, is a renewable, indeed, an inexhaustible resource. The energies he sought to channel are born anew in every person.

Neither is the wisdom of the republican tradition spent. Machiavelli recognized that the task of virtue was to create its own context, a *vivere civile*, and it is that undertaking I would urge in conclusion.

But modern republics are large representative democracies, with huge bureaucracies, public and private. Scale presents real problems. One cannot conduct daily plebiscites; it is not just socialism, as in Oscar Wilde's witticism, that takes too many evenings, but liberty itself. And even if time were not precious, political results are often exasperatingly incommensurate with effort. And conduct would not be virtuous, in the sense I wish to use it, if it were ineffectual—or deluded.

Take, for example, public education. Educated parents, if they are also prosperous, will attend just so many inconclusive school committee meetings, before they opt out of the public schools altogether. They have insured that their own children will read *The Odyssey* and *Middlemarch*, but they must still encounter and often rely upon the graduates—or the drop-outs—of the schools they have abandoned: producing or not producing goods, providing or failing to provide services, voting for demagogues or not voting at all, holding up convenience stores.

One can not opt out of the public realm nor through the most ambitious privatization eliminate the public consequences of private acts. How then might one think about education as a common problem? There seem two drastically different, but equally republican, possibilities. One might, in the interests of democratic accountability, concentrate authority. Do away with elected school boards, place significantly enhanced authority in the hands of appointed officials responsible to, say, an elected mayor or governor, and let the public vote up or down on the results. Or, one might, in the interests of democratic participation, diffuse authority: decentralize, multiply the pressure points, maximize civic involvement.

I advocate neither course. But I think we must accustom ourselves, as we address common problems, to concern ourselves not only with their solutions but also with the ways—the institutions and procedures—through which the solutions are sought. "The only way out is through," Robert Frost said, about the trials of daily life. I recommend that proceduralism.

NOTES

1. Tocqueville, *Democracy in America*, Book II, 525.
2. Pieper, *The Four Cardinal Virtues*, 6.
3. Harvey Mansfield makes this point in his introduction to Machiavelli, *The Prince*.
4. Machiavelli, *The Prince*, 61.
5. *Ibid.*, 103.
6. Machiavelli, *Discourses*, 113.
7. *Ibid.*, 114-115.
8. *Ibid.*, 302.
9. *Ibid.*, 194.
10. *Ibid.*, 124.
11. Machiavelli, *Florentine Histories*, 276.
12. Machiavelli, *Discourses*, 124.
13. Montesquieu, *Considérations*, 453.
14. *Ibid.*
15. Montesquieu, *L'Esprit*, 544.
16. *Ibid.*, 542.
17. *Ibid.*, 538-41.
18. *Ibid.*
19. *Ibid.*
20. La Rochefoucauld, *Maximes*, 56, 8-9, 3.
21. Hirschman, *The Passions and the Interests*, 9.
22. La Rochefoucauld, *op. cit.*, 142.
23. Smith, *The Theory of Moral Sentiments*, 417.
24. La Rochefoucauld, *op. cit.*, 28.

25. Smith, *Moral Sentiments*, 166.
26. Steuart, *Principles of Political Oeconomy*, 242-244.
27. *Ibid.*
28. Smith, *op. cit.*, 154.
29. Hume, *Hume's Ethical Writings*, 65-66.
30. Rousseau, *Discours sur l'origine de l'inégalité*, 162.
31. Smith, *op. cit.*, 47; *ibid.*, 195.
32. Smith, *op. cit.*, 69.
33. *Ibid.*, 293.
34. Mandeville, *Inquiry into the Origins of Honour*, 38.
35. *Ibid.*, 83-84.
36. Hannah Arendt, *On Revolution*, 75-76.
37. Rousseau, *Contrat social*, 33.
38. *Ibid.*, 43.
39. Smith, *The Wealth of Nations*, 384-385. Tocqueville, *Democracy in America*, 9.
40. Smith, *Wealth of Nations*, 734-740.
41. Anthyme Corbon quoted in Auspitz, *The Radical Bourgeoisie*, 32.
42. *Ibid.*
43. Tocqueville, *Souvenirs*, 152.
44. Tocqueville, *Democracy in America*, 527.
45. *Ibid.*, 515.
46. J.S. Mill, *Considerations on Representative Government*, 188.
47. Mill, *On the Subjection of Women*, 455.
48. Arendt, *op. cit.*, 53-110. Professor Benjamin I. Schwartz, in *Dissent*, 1970, offers learned and, I think, irrefutable criticism of Miss Arendt's political writings.
49. Alasdair MacIntyre, *After Virtue*, 8, 236-237, 262-263.

SELECTED BIBLIOGRAPHY

Hirschman, Albert O. *The Passions and the Interests*. Princeton: Princeton University Press, 1977.

_____. *Rival Views of Market Society*. New York: Viking Press, 1986.

Hume, David. *Essays, Moral, Political and Literary*. Indianapolis: Liberty Classics, 1985.

La Rochefoucauld. *Réflections ou sentences et Maximes morales*. Paris: Classiques Garnier, 1961.

Machiavelli, Niccolò. *The Discourses*. Translated by Leslie J. Walker. S.J. New York: Penguin Books, 1970.

_____. *Florentine Histories*. Translated by Laura Banfield and Harvey C. Mansfield, Jr. Princeton: Princeton University Press, 1988.

_____. *The Prince*. Translated by Harvey C. Mansfield, Jr. Chicago: The University of Chicago Press, 1985.

Mandeville, Bernard. *An Inquiry in to Origins of Honour*. London: John Brotherton, 1732.

Mill, John Stuart. *Three Essays*. Oxford: Oxford University Press, 1975.

Montesquieu, Charles Secondat, Baron de. *Oeuvres complètes*. Paris: Editions de Seuil, 1964.

Pieper, Josef. *The Four Cardinal Virtues*. South Bend: Notre Dame Press, 1966.

Rousseau, Jean-Jacques. *Political Writings*. Edited by Charles Vaughan. Oxford: Basil Blackwell, 1962.

Smith, Adam. *The Theory of Moral Sentiments*. Indianapolis: Liberty Classics, 1970.

_____. *The Wealth of Nations*. New York: Modern Library, 1937.

Steuart, Sir James. *An Inquiry into the Principles of Political Economy*. Edited by Andrew S. Skinner. Chicago: University of Chicago, 1966.

Tocqueville, Alexis de. *Democracy in America*. Edited by J.P. Mayer. New York: Anchor Books, 1969.

_____. *Souvenirs*. Paris: Gallimard, 1964.

COMMENTARY

Arendt, Hannah. *On Revolution*. New York: The Viking Press, 1965.

MacIntyre, Alasdair. *Beyond Virtue*. Second Edition. Notre Dame, Indiana: University of Notre Dame Press, 1984.

Pocock, J.G.A. *The Machiavellian Moment*. Princeton: Princeton University Press, 1975.

Schwartz, Benjamin I. "The Politics of Hannah Arendt." *Dissent*. 1970.

THREE

RIGHTS, CITIZENSHIP, AND CIVILITY

Robert A. Goldwin

Two great difficulties beset liberal democratic societies, and both have to do with the rights of individuals. The first stems from the tension between rights and democracy, the second from the tension between rights and citizenship. Neither is a new or recent problem, neither is avoidable; both are inherent in the very idea of the liberal democratic society. The chief subjects of this essay are the significance of these two fundamental difficulties and their consequences for the present status and future prospects of liberal democratic societies.

THE TENSION BETWEEN RIGHTS AND DEMOCRACY

When we speak of liberal democratic societies rather than democratic societies simply, we make an important distinction. There is an obvious difference between democracy and liberal democracy; not every democratic society is liberal. Democracy means rule by the majority. Majority rule may not be the whole story of democracy, but surely it is the essence of it. Democratic majorities can be illiberal and even tyrannical. Tyranny of the majority is one of the worst dangers liberal democracies must guard against. Those who understand that an unrestrained majority is as capable of tyranny as are oligarchs or monarchs strive to make our democratic societies nondespotic, respectful of the rights of individuals and minorities—to make them, in a word, liberal.

A liberal society, whether democratic or not, strives to protect the rights of subjects or citizens, that is, the rights of every individual and any minority from abuse, especially by the ruling power, wherever that power may reside. A liberal democratic society, therefore, protects individuals and minorities from the power of the ruling majority. Thus we see that in a liberal democratic society the powers of the majority must be limited; there are some things the majority cannot be permitted to do. That imperative of liberal democracy finds expression in the very first words of the American Bill of Rights, "Congress shall make no law" on the following several subjects,[1] to make it clear that whatever the democratic majority might wish its representatives to do, some powers to act are denied to them.

A liberal democratic society must find ways, consistent with majority rule (or else it ceases to be democratic), to restrain the powers of the majority, which means that the majority must restrain itself, for other than the majority there is no political source of restraining power in a democracy. In short, liberal democracy must be constitutional democracy, the whole society constituting itself so that the majority, acting on behalf of the whole society, consents to and imposes binding limits on its own powers.

But a democratic majority is unlikely to succeed in self-denial in an effective, consistent, and persisting fashion unless the constitutional devices for protecting rights are uncommonly prudent, powerful, and to some extent self-enforcing. The Madisonian model is the one that comes first to mind, for James Madison was the first to expound the arguments for devices to promote energetic majority rule while limiting the powers of the majority to engage in abuses against the rights of the people. He was not an advocate of weak government. He sought, rather, a formula for effective majority rule capable of doing good things, while weakened or incapacitated for doing bad things.[2]

The first device was to form a union of diverse elements over a sizable enough territory so that there would be regional and economic varieties of interests. Both parts—union and diversity—were essential. Too much diversity, or diversity of the wrong kind, makes community difficult, if not impossible. There must be a common bond to hold the entire nation together, shared principles, sentiments, and interests powerful enough to combat the divisive tendencies of different peoples and different regions to break off in order to further parochial interests. If the bonds of union are strong enough, then diversity, even a multiplicity of interests, regions, commercial pursuits, and religious sects is beneficial for protecting rights, because the multiplicity of interests renders the majority less dangerous. The great danger of majority rule becoming tyrannical lies in the formation of a permanent or persisting majority. If the majority is always being formed and reformed by shifting elements, coming together and breaking apart as the issues change, the danger of such majorities to rights is greatly diminished.[3]

Shifting, impermanent majorities produce many desirable consequences for the security of rights. Members of the minority on one issue have the encouraging prospect of being part of the majority on another issue. Since citizens and elected officials know that their opponent on one issue may well be their ally on the next issue, they develop habits of restraint in seeking voting victories, and are inclined to consider compromises and modifications that lessen the defeats of possible future allies. They learn it is good policy to be considerate of the other's interests as much as possible, and they expect the same in return. It becomes easier to see the danger to your rights in the proposed abuse of the rights of another, and thus to have reason to avoid it. Habits of public moderation with respect to rights are thus probable consequences of constitutional devices to discourage formation of a permanent majority.

The Madisonian devices also include separation of powers and federalism, which have the effect of making a concentration of political power difficult, if not impossible, by establishing numerous lesser centers of power. Here again the idea is not weak government, but government with numerous centers of power, capable of getting things done, yet not capable of running roughshod over the rights of individuals or minorities. The power to make laws is separate from the power to execute them, and the judicial power is separate from both. The separation is maintained in design and in practice by admixture: that is, the executive has a share in the legislative power by means of a partial veto of legislation; the legislative branch has a share in the executive power by a voice in executive and judicial appointments; and the judiciary has a share in both by its power of judicial review. By sharing powers, each branch is able to defend its separate status against encroachments by the others. And since the state governments are designed very much on the same patterns, the dispersion of powers is increased and extended.

A vigorous and diversified private sector, regulated but not owned by the government, is also part of the Madisonian scheme, including not only commerce of every description but also the press, the only private industry with its very own constitutional amendment to shield it from acts of Congress. Because the voting public holds the president and the Congress responsible for the state of the economy, the government always leans toward business regulation; but the private sector of business is so vast, so complex, and so resistant to effective control that there is also a strong inclination to keep hands off in order not to stifle the inherent vitality of private enterprise. A prosperous people who are for the most part not employees of the government or dependent on it in other ways for their livelihood, and therefore independent enough to be able to defend their own rights, by and large, are another element of the Madisonian scheme for providing for security of rights under a democratic majority. (To the extent that more Americans are becoming dependent on government, in one way or another, for their livelihood, this precaution against excessive government power endangering rights is diminished.)

The constitutional provisions that protect the free exercise of religion, prohibit the establishment of an official national religion, and prohibit a religious test for employment by the government,[4] combined with the multiplicity of religious sects that has always existed in the United States and constantly increases, add greatly to the maintenance of the rights of religious freedom. There is always a kind of religious turmoil throughout the country and always evidence of the universal tendencies of religious hostility and persecution; but in the end there is remarkably little violation of religious rights, and when the hostility does evidence itself in actions, the courts are rarely reluctant to act to protect the free exercise of religion.

The greatest failure of the Madisonian scheme has been in the protection of the rights of racial groups, especially, of course, black

Americans. Madison recognized that the prior existence of slavery was the greatest obstacle to making a union under the Constitution; slavery introduced a contradictory flaw, nearly a fatal flaw as it turned out, that could not be resolved constitutionally, perhaps because there was not a sufficient multiplicity of interests with regard to slavery and race. The pro-slavery representation in the Congress formed a persisting bloc that was not susceptible to compromise or moderation. It did not shift, ever, on that single issue. The continuation and spread of slavery was, in the end, more important to the pro-slavery forces than union, and so the Madisonian scheme did not apply.

That exception to diversity within union as the means of restraining the majority from violating the rights of the minority, consistent with majority rule, only emphasizes the fact that although a sound constitution can cope with the difficulty raised by the tension between rights and democracy, it can never be resolved completely or finally. The continuing inherent tension means unending struggle, but the struggle, so long as it remains within constitutional bounds, is not a reason for discouragement about the present and future prospects of liberal democratic societies. What is required is a continuing tolerance for a high level of dispute, disagreement, uncertainty, disappointment, and frustration—and an understanding that that is the price we pay for the extraordinary benefits of constitutionalism.

THE TENSION BETWEEN RIGHTS AND CITIZENSHIP

The second difficulty of democratic liberal societies, stemming from the tension between rights and citizenship, is of a different kind and not likely to be resolved by constitutional devices.

Liberal societies declare that all human beings have rights and that the chief function of government is to secure these rights. The oldest of the political-rights doctrines held that individual rights are natural and inherent in every human being, but theoretical formulations concerning natural rights have been out of favor for a long time. We now avoid calling rights natural and speak instead of human rights, civil rights, and political rights, and defend them with fervor and determination; most advocates of rights avoid speculation about where they come from. But whether they assert or deny that rights are natural, political societies based on the rights of the individual have many characteristics in common, chief among them the principle that the government exists to serve the individual.

In a rights-based society, the individual comes first, not the community. The rights of the individual are powerful, masterful, and primary. In comparison, all things relating to community, including the obligations of citizenship, are weak, servile, and derivative. The older terminology, which did not hesitate to speak of the naturalness of rights, expressed it more forcefully: individual rights are powerful because they are a natural part of us; the community, and everything linked to the community, including citizenship, are not a natural part of us, but are acquired, are artificial. From that difference stems an imbalance of the powers of rights and duties in liberal democratic societies, a tension between natural rights and unnatural citizenship.

It is possible to make the argument as to the dominance of rights over the duties of citizenship without relying on the theoretical "naturalness" of rights, but the discussion is greatly impoverished by avoiding the term. What does it mean to speak of the naturalness or unnaturalness of citizenship? The word *natural* had fundamentally different meanings for Plato or Aristotle, on the one hand, and Locke on the other. When the ancients spoke of the nature of man, they meant what a human being could be or would be in completion or fulfillment of what we nowadays would call his full "potential." They did not mean, however, the varying potential of one or another particular individual human being, but rather the realization of what it means to be a human being. If we could imagine a person, not a superman, fully human in every admirable respect, that person would represent their understanding of human nature.[5] The political significance of this understanding was that this desired realization of the good man was possible only in the circumstances of life in a good political community, although they would add that the fully developed human being would transcend the life of the citizen and the polis, to live the contemplative life, the life of the mind. Transcendence of the political community, however, would be possible only as a consequence of life in a well-governed political community, and with its fullest assistance.[6]

The word *natural* meant something quite different for Locke. Natural for him was what anything is before being altered by man's artifice. What is wild and uncultivated is natural. Uncultivated land he called land "left to nature." Natural is the way we would be if never exposed to education and cultural habituation. Natural for Locke is not the end or completion of a process to develop the fullness of humanity, but the undistorted beginning, the raw stuff. "Doin' what comes natcher'ly," as the song goes; that is, behavior uninfluenced by rules, customs, and traditions is what Locke has in mind. It is in this sense of natural that he says it is natural for man to be without government.[7]

Perhaps the strongest example of what Locke meant by natural is revealed near the beginning of his discussion of the education of children. Locke says that child rearing has two parts, care of the body and care of the mind, and the aim is to achieve "a sound mind in a sound body."[8] He deals first with the physical development of the child, discussing such matters as exercise, clothing, sleep, diet, and finally, "Going to Stool regularly." "People that are very loose," Locke says, "have seldom strong thoughts, or strong bodies." But it is to the treatment of "the contrary Evil," "costiveness" or constipation, without resorting to the use of laxatives, that Locke, speaking as a physician advising parents how to avoid calling in the doctor, devotes greater attention and study. In the ensuing discussion, in the space of less than two pages, we encounter these phrases: "the benefit of Nature," "Sollicite Nature," "put Nature upon her Duty," "sure to have Nature very obedient," "those Motions of Nature," "a requisite easing of Nature,"—all to describe the proper method of developing a youngster's regularity of bowel movements.[9] That, for Locke, was nature. And in that sense of the word, Locke meant that citizenship is not natural.

What is natural for us is not to act as citizens but to act as individuals, with our own personal concerns and interests foremost, as in the state of nature, that is, without government, without attention to the good of others. Locke could say, "I think it is every man's indispensable duty, to do all the service he can to his country,"[10] but that is not the same as saying that doing your public duty comes naturally; in fact, his thoughts concerning education are necessary because doing what is right as citizen, and even as parent, does not come naturally.

Rights are powerful. Duties, the duties of citizenship, are not powerful. We tend to shirk them, most of us, if we can. They must be inculcated; they require instruction and even exhortation; in most societies failure to perform citizen duties results in punishments. And in a liberal society, devoted to the practice of liberty, it is difficult to discipline people or indoctrinate them in authoritarian ways. Developing a sense of duty, of obligation to the community, of public service, and then getting performance of those duties, presents obvious difficulties in a liberal society.

In ancient teachings about political community, such as Aristotle's *Politics*, individual human beings were not considered self-sufficient, as whole or complete in themselves; only as members of the political community did they have the prospect of becoming fully human, of living a suitably human life. To live outside a political community was unnatural, not consistent with the nature of a human being. The natural condition of a human being was to be a member of the political community, to be a citizen.[11] Nowhere in the writings of Plato and Aristotle is there discussion of rights, whether called natural, human, civil, or political. The language of rights was not part of their political vocabulary. It was not evident to them that governments are established to secure the rights of individuals. Political communities are established because human beings need political community in order to be human, not just for the sake of life but for the sake of the good life.[12] In that sense men are political animals; the good life, a life in accord with human nature, can be realized only as part of a political community. The natural state for human beings is the polis. Without it we are something other than human.

The assumptions and arguments of the Declaration of Independence differ fundamentally from that ancient teaching. The underlying theory of the Declaration is that our rights are inherent and natural and therefore independent of political society. The source of this assertion is to be found in the state of nature writings of several authors, but especially of John Locke. The argument is that the natural condition of human beings is not to live as citizens of a political community but as individuals without government.[13] This is not the place to rehearse in detail or even summarize the teachings of Locke; suffice it to say that when Locke spoke of the state of nature he did not mean that he thought human beings had ever lived without government for long periods of time, but he did say and mean seriously that though men are found everywhere living in political communities, citizenship is not natural to them. At those infrequent and brief moments when men do find themselves in the natural condition—in times of upheaval, as a consequence of anarchy or the extremes of despotic rule—without community or government, they are "quickly driven into society" by the harshness of the natural condition;[14] but that does not alter Locke's teaching that civil society is not the natural state. Civil society is a human invention, an improvement on the natural condition, something we make as a welcome alternative to the uncertain dangers of the state of nature, a man-made improvement on the poor job nature did for us. Once in civil society, since we are not prepared by nature to be citizens, the attributes of citizenship must be acquired.

Societies influenced by Locke, which means many liberal democracies, start with individual human beings and their rights as given, and from that given they must build the community. The ancient polis, and many modern political societies that are not really based on the the primacy of the rights of the individual (despite their hypocritical use of the rhetoric of rights), start with the community and derive the duties of citizenship and what they call rights from the nature and needs of the community. These political societies do not have the same kind of problem with citizenship that liberal societies have, and rights have in them a completely different status and are of a different sort. They are not natural, inherent, and inalienable. They are derivative, privileges granted to individuals by the community for the convenience of the community. The so-called rights in such a community would be more accurately acknowledged to be benefits bestowed by the government for a price, on condition of performance of civic duties, with the understanding that they will be withdrawn by the same authorities who granted them if there is dissatisfaction with the citizens' behavior.

In short, as we all know, the tension between rights and citizenship can be removed by eliminating liberal democracy. The tension exists only in societies where the individual comes first and where society is understood to exist for the sake of securing individual rights. The question is whether there is a way to resolve the tension between rights and citizenship within a liberal democratic society.

THE PUBLIC REALM AND THE PRIVATE REALM

In a political community based on the primacy of the rights of the individual, the distinction as to what is public and what is private is fundamental. The pledge to provide security for personal rights means that there are some major human activities and concerns that are beyond the legitimate reach of government, some things that are just none of the government's business. The meaning of the first ten amendments to the Constitution, beginning with the five magnificent words of denial, "Congress shall make no law," is that the legitimate powers of government do not reach to religion, speech, press, and so on. The imperative for the security of rights is that these fundamentally important human activities, which are also citizen activities because they concern the whole community, are nevertheless none of the government's business. In practice, of course, because these activities are of such importance not only to individuals but also to the community as a whole, it turns out that they cannot be kept completely beyond the government's reach. Some government action is found to be necessary, to limit or prohibit libelous speech, perjury, obscenity, shouting "fire" in a crowded theater when there is no fire, and "fighting words," to give just a few examples. Even given numerous exceptions, the principle that governmental powers are not to be exercised in these matters governs, restricts, and limits what the government can legitimately do. Limited government means that certain very important powers are denied to government, and limited government, constitutionalism, is what we are talking about when we speak of liberal democratic societies.

Totalitarian rule, the opposite of limited government, is characterized by an old formulation: "Where the law is silent, there you are forbidden." The meaning is that political power reaches to the totality of human activity; public authority governs every aspect of your life. There is no separation of private and public. Any moments of freedom are exceptions, and these exceptions must be authorized, which means that they are not private moments. If such an extension of authority seems farfetched, we need only think of familiar nonpolitical examples, such as the situation of young children, or soldiers under strict military discipline, or convicts in prison, or anyone to whom it would be reasonable to say in a commanding or menacing tone, "Who said you could do that?"

That rhetorical question conveys exactly the message of totalitarian rule, that there is no realm of private freedom, that all your thoughts and actions are subject to public power, that you are not in charge of yourself, that you may do only what someone else says you may do.

It is quite the opposite in a society whose government has been limited by the fundamental distinction of what is public and what is private. In such a society the rule is, "Where the law is silent, there you are free." The difference was well expressed by a photographer who prepared a book on details of the daily personal life of ordinary people throughout the United States, and, subsequently, a similar book on daily life in the Soviet Union (prior to *glasnost*). When asked in a radio interview whether he experienced difficulties in getting permission to take certain photographs, he compared the countries this way: "In the United States, it was yes until someone said no. In the Soviet Union, it was no until someone said yes."

The first principle of liberal societies is the assertion of the existence of rights as an essential attribute of the human person. The sequence of reasoning proceeds from that starting point. The protection of rights requires society and government, but because unrestrained government poses a threat to the security of rights, government's powers must be limited to those necessary to protect rights, or at least to those that do not threaten rights. Some things are therefore none of the government's business, and government must be made to keep its hands off them. The things that are the government's business are in the public realm; the rest are in the private realm. And the private realm is a realm of personal freedom.

CIVILITY: THE REALM BETWEEN

Despite the line I have drawn, the division of public and private is not sharp, and the separation not at all complete. The private realm includes not only things that are none of the government's business but also things that are of deep concern to the whole community.

We do not speak of law enforcement in the private realm, but there are sanctions and restraints of a different sort concerning things that are "just not done." The private realm is the realm of the "unenforceable," but it is not lacking in rules and constraints.

Many words testify to the existence of violators of the rules of the private realm: liar, cheat, phony, charlatan, bigot, hypocrite, philanderer, double-dealer, four-flusher, two-timer, cad (admittedly, many of these have an old-fashioned sound). They indicate unacceptable behavior that is usually not criminal, that is therefore not punishable by law, but that does break well-known rules and is hurtful to others. Hearts are broken, reputations are ruined, lives are disrupted, savings are lost; and yet as important as the consequences may be to persons affected by this form of wrongdoing, in our modern liberal democratic societies it is not a matter of public concern unless laws are violated.

There are forms of private wrongdoing, however, that have an important public effect and blur the separation between public and private. For example, on many leading American college campuses there is an increase of "harassment by vilification," described by columnist Nat Hentoff as "vicious and deeply wounding words aimed at blacks, women, and homosexuals."[15] This intensifying barrage of offensive speech has led several law student associations on leading campuses to call for restrictions on student speech and press. These student organizations would ordinarily be staunch advocates of protection for all freedoms, and especially freedoms of speech and press, but the students are so oppressed by the verbal attacks that they are seeking relief by asking for sanctions against the unprovoked verbal denunciations heaped on them relentlessly as they try innocently to get on with their studies. Support for freedom of speech is clearly related to conditions of public civility and perhaps even dependent on such conditions.

From many parts of the world there are reports every day of such hatred between groups of fellow citizens—Armenians and Azerbaijanis in the Soviet Union, Catholics and Protestants in Northern Ireland, Hindus and Muslims in India, Tamils and Sinhalese in Sri Lanka, to give just a few examples—that they attack each other, physically, as enemies, with many injured and killed. In such situations, there must be a strong police or military presence on the streets to attempt to preserve the peace. There cannot be domestic tranquility under such conditions; but there can be, at best, a suppression of violence by the exercise of superior force by the police, acting on behalf of the community as a whole.

Similarly, as the actions of the offensive students make clear, when there is intense verbal abuse against groups because of race, religion, nationality, or language, it becomes difficult, if not impossible, to maintain the principle and the practice of freedom of speech. At what point this level of public incivility and freedom of speech become incompatible may be hard to determine precisely, but surely we can say that the less public civility, the greater the difficulty of maintaining freedom of speech, because in the absence of civility, community force is needed to do what is otherwise accomplished by uncoerced law-abidingness.

From the public standpoint, freedom of speech is most important for the protection it provides for unpopular, disquieting, even abhorrent speech. Protection of speech is most important for the offensive speech most of us would rather not have to hear. But that makes it clear that the conditions must be such that there is among the citizenry, and among those with official responsibilities, a high degree of tolerance for the expression of unwelcome views, on the one hand, and a certain restraint and prudence on the part of dissenters in presenting their unpleasant messages, on the other hand, which tolerance and restraint are both an obvious aspect of public civility.

Not every people is capable of allegiance to freedom of speech, press, religion, or assembly—an assertion that tends to surprise many persons of good intentions and worthy aspirations for humanity, despite the fact that examples of that truth are encountered again and again in many parts of the world. In many societies, for instance those where religious piety dominates the life of the citizens, there is no tolerance for nonbelievers or adherents to other religious faiths. Freedom of religion is not a concept they know or tolerate. They lack the acceptance of the necessary principles to support the free exercise of religion and it is fruitless to expect that such tolerance will prevail there. In short, if a certain kind of public civility is lacking, civil rights cannot be secured.

But the American students who are offended by the vicious verbal attacks on groups, and the university officials who agree with them, seem to think the solution lies in putting restrictions on offensive speech. The University of Michigan adopted a code in 1988, subsequently struck down in Federal District Court after being challenged by the American Civil Liberties Union, that would have banned "any behavior, verbal or physical, that stigmatizes or victimizes an individual on the basis of race, ethnicity, religion, sex, sexual orientation, creed, national origin, ancestry, age, marital status, handicap, or Vietnam-era veteran status...."[16] Despite their laudable intentions, the proponents of such a provision are acting on the unsound and dangerous conviction that civility can be restored and freedom enjoyed by methods of enforcement. What may mislead them is that up to a point, that may be true. But there is grave danger in persisting in that direction, in seeking to secure rights by making enforceable laws restricting offensive speech. That is the harsh truth that the authors of the American Bill of Rights saw so clearly.

The point is set out starkly in the opening words of the First Amendment: "Congress shall make no law" abridging the freedom of speech and press. Why does it not say that "Congress shall make laws" to protect those rights? Would that not be more direct, more affirmative, more effective? That is what the students and university officials are advocating, and that is what many constitution-writers in other countries, ever since 1791, have undertaken. Why not?

The reasoning of Madison and his colleagues is that such rights are endangered not only by groups attacking groups, but more so by the overwhelming powers of public officials. Innumerable examples throughout history, right down to the present moment, attest to the fact that government power is the greatest threat—always potentially, often actually—to individual rights. The secret of securing the rights of individuals is to deny power to government to interfere with the private realm. To say that the government shall make no laws on this subject is a denial of power; to say that the government shall make laws on this subject is an accretion of power. That is the reasoning that guided them. What has arguably been the world's most effective instrument of constitutional protection of rights, the Constitution of the United States, as amended, has a short list of rights in no way comprehensive, negative in form, lacking completely in guarantees, and with no mention of duties. It does not seem far-fetched to me that there is a connection between the prudent restraint inherent in the negative form of what the American founders did and the successful results.

But without some remedial action, the students are still left unprotected against hurtful verbal abuse, with no recourse. The fact is that even if government is the chief threat to the rights of individuals, it is not the only threat. In countries all over the world, including liberal democratic societies, groups devote themselves determinedly to abusing the rights of others, often with as much violence as they can muster. And that situation makes us wonder what the conditions are that make it possible for the freedoms of speech, press, religion, and assembly to be sustained.

If there were academic leaders who were respected and considered authoritative to advise students that abusive racial attacks are not acceptable behavior on the campus of an institution devoted to genuine pursuit of the truth, then no new restrictive laws would be required. If young people were brought up to observe the rules of civility that command consideration for the beliefs of others and tolerance for different ways of conducting one's life, then formal regulation of behavior would not be necessary. In one sense the solution to the problem is easy and obvious: people, even young people, should know how to behave themselves, should know that there are certain rules that are helpful in living together in civil society, and that these rules are even more important for pursuing together the work of a university. After all, there was a time when universities were spoken of as "the public nurseries of religion, piety, learning, and civility." But today expectations of civility on university campuses seem unrealistic. Why should that be? Why can we not expect that the exhortations of respected academic leaders will be forthcoming and effective?

The reason, I think, leads us to the central difficulty of liberal democratic societies. There is little or nothing in the doctrines of liberalism or democracy that has to do with public propriety. In every society there is encouragement for citizens to do their duty and to be civic-minded, but the content of it does not come from liberal or democratic teachings. Those teachings emphasize the welfare of the individual, not the common welfare. The fact is that liberal democratic societies are not purely so, but all have a heavy admixture of other kinds of regimes, with principles unrelated and often contradictory to the principles of liberal democracy. The principles of duty, honor, public service, sacrifice, charity, patriotism, respect for elders, respect for authority, all have their sources in other times, other regimes, other ways of thinking about civil society. These vestiges of other systems of political community have persisted among us, as a kind of residue, and have made liberal democracy sustainable, until now. But increasingly we are seeing that liberal democracy does not have the teachings to sustain these older, foreign principles, and so we see disruptions for which we seem to have no remedies—divorce, illegitimacy, drug abuse, child abuse, private and public corruption, violent crime, and a general deterioration of public civility.

When the United States was founded, the leading statesmen were advocates of constitutional liberal democracy; they were also gentlemen—not scholars, but learned—well schooled in the teachings of the ancients. Gentlemen were then the repositories within themselves of the wisdom, customs, and traditions handed down from other times and ways of life. They established a new form of political society, but it was not wholly new because it did not eradicate the old standards of behavior. It relied on them, perhaps more than was realized.

Today those old forms of conduct are all but lost. We have no gentlemen, but we have men of means who could be thought of as a rough equivalent. We also have a learned class, our academics, but they too are only the roughest sort of equivalent, because they do not consider it their role to guide the civil behavior of the society. There is no one in sight likely to undertake the task of developing that level of public civility essential to the maintenance of individual rights. There lies the gravest danger to the future of democratic liberal societies.

NOTES

1. "Congress shall make no law respecting an establishment of religion, or prohibiting the free exercise thereof; or abridging the freedom of speech, or of the press; or the right of the people peaceably to assemble, and to petition the Government for a redress of grievances." The Constitution of the United States of America, First Amendment.
2. Alexander Hamilton, James Madison, and John Jay, *The Federalist*, ed. Jacob E. Cooke (Cleveland and New York: World Publishing Company, 1961), no. 51.
3. *Ibid.*, no. 10.
4. Article VI of the Constitution provides that "no religious test shall ever be required as a qualification to any office or public trust under the United States."
5. Aristotle, *Politics*, Book I, 1252b.

6. Aristotle, *Nicomachean Ethics*, Book X, 1179b.

7. John Locke, *Two Treatises of Government*, ed. Peter Laslett (New York and Toronto: The New American Library, 1965), Second Treatise, chapters II and V.

8. John Locke, *Some Thoughts Concerning Education* in *The Educational Writings of John Locke*, ed. James L. Axtell (Cambridge: At the University Press, 1968), sec. 1: 114.

9. *Ibid.*, secs. 23-28: 133-136.

10. *Ibid.*, Prefatory Letter, 111.

11. Aristotle, *Politics*, Book I, 1253a.

12. *Ibid*, 1252b.

13. Locke, Second Treatise, ch. II, sec. 4.

14. *Ibid.*, ch. IX, sec. 127; see also ch. II, sec. 13 and ch. IX, secs. 123-126.

15. "When Good People Punish Bad Speech," *The Washington Post*, May 27, 1989, 26.

16. *AGB Reports* (published by the Association of Governing Boards of Colleges and Universities), January/February 1990, 6-14.

FOUR

CIVILITY AND CITIZENSHIP IN THE AMERICAN FOUNDING

Charles R. Kesler

The general problem of civility and citizenship may be stated succinctly. It is not at all unusual for countries to have citizenship without the restraints of civility; nor is it surprising to find examples of civility among men who are not united by formal ties of citizenship. But how is it possible to combine civility and citizenship in healthy and mutually reinforcing ways?

To be "civil" in ordinary usage means to be polite, respectful, decent. It is a quality implying, in particular, the restraint of anger directed towards others, whether fellow passengers, siblings, or citizens. In this sense, it is not the same thing as warmth and indeed implies a certain coolness: civility helps to cool the too hot passions of citizenship or of a certain kind of citizenship. From this thought, however, it is only a small step to a different and higher view of civility as something positive, rather than negative. In this light, civility seems to correspond to that concord or *homonoia* that Aristotle identified as characteristic of political friendship.[1] When citizens are civil to one another, despite their political disagreement, they reveal that these disagreements are less important than their resolution to remain fellow citizens. They agree, or, as Aristotle would put it, are of the same mind on the fundamental political questions, even if they differ on secondary issues. Without this fundamental agreement reflected in civility, citizenship would be self-contradictory and finally self-destructive; it would be civil war by another name.

For the sake of its own perfection, citizenship requires civility, or more precisely, the concord of opinions underlying civility. The French Revolution remains the unforgettable modern example of citizenship's self-destruction in the absence of such a harmony of views and affections. Citizen Brissot, Citizen Danton, Citizen Robespierre—one by one they fell victims to ever more radical and ever more exclusive definitions of the good citizen. Tyranny itself is the process of exclusion carried to its logical extreme, in which a permanent civil war may be said to exist between the tyrant, on the one hand, and his oppressed people, on the other. So far as the tyrant is concerned, of course, he is the sole citizen: he is the state.

Still it would be a great mistake to believe that the opposite of tyranny or of permanent civil war, whether explicit or implicit, is simply a concord of opinion. Political friendship can be based on better or worse opinions. The criteria for evaluating them must therefore be extrinsic to the opinions themselves. In other words, even as citizenship requires civility, so civility points beyond itself to certain permanent and objective moral standards—to the nature of "civil government," and, higher still, to the moral and theoretical concerns of what is rightly called civilization.

Needless to say, these terms—citizenship, civility, civilization—are cognates, deriving from the Latin *civis* (citizen) and *civitas* (city), which are themselves the Latin equivalents of the Greek family of words stemming from *polis* (city). From the classical point of view, the civilized are those fit to live in cities, fit to bear the burdens and enjoy the fruits of citizenship, that is ruling and being ruled in turn. Those who are not civilized, who are not political, properly so called, are barbarians. Greek popular opinion did not hesitate to label as barbarians all who were non-Greek; but on that point philosophical opinion demurred. Aristotle, for instance, preferred Carthage as an example of a well governed non-Greek city.[2] Despite what might be called the openness of the philosophical viewpoint, the city—not "civilization," a word neither the Greeks nor the Romans used, and certainly not "civilizations"—remained the focus of classical political science. But the relation of the city to civilization, and thus the focus of political science, changed dramatically after the advent of Christianity. This is important for the case of America, as I will try to make clear in due course.

To look at civility and citizenship in the American founding is a rather different task from examining them in liberal democracy as a whole. The American Founders spoke (*inter alia*) of popular government, democracy, republicanism, free government, and civil government, but not, so far as I know, of liberal democracy. This is a more recent term, applied in this century to everything from Weimar Germany to contemporary India. Indeed it is a serious question whether thinking mainly in terms of the genus "liberal democracy" does not distract us from what is more distinctive and valuable and, in truth, generally relevant about the American political experience—the sort of things that kept and continue to keep the United States from going the way of Weimar Germany. Let two examples suffice. The "veneration" of or "reverence" for the law, above all for the Constitution, spoken of in *Federalist* 49 and confirmed by observers of America from Tocqueville to Robert Bellah, is not part of traditional liberal democratic theory, at least if Hobbes, Spinoza, and Locke are taken as representative. Similarly, the very notion of "founding" or "Founding Fathers," in the American sense of those terms, is absent from the horizon of liberal democratic theory. The social contract, understood simply as a by-product of individual calculation or utility maximization, is almost the antithesis of a real founding, as Plato, Aristotle, and Cicero knew long before, and better than, Rousseau, whose treatment of the problem has become famous.

Given these and other reasons, I think it is sensible to look at the problem of civility and citizenship in the American founding primarily in the light of what is distinctive to the founding. This is not to deny that the United States was intended to be an example unto the nations. But it was intended to be an example of republicanism, purer and nobler than any previous incarnation, precisely because it was to be founded explicitly and proudly on the rights of man as man, rights whose title derived from the "laws of Nature and of Nature's God." Broadly speaking, the American Founders thought of themselves as perfecting the tradition of republicanism, of rescuing liberty, equality, and the rule of law from their more or less imperfect embodiments in previous republics. Yet in invoking "nature's God"—who was also the living God to whom they appealed for the rectitude of their intentions—the Founders acknowledged a world changed, in vital respects, by the presence of Christianity. In these circumstances, the republican cause had to be thought through again in light of the conflicts and potential harmony between reason and biblical revelation.

There is nothing more distinctive, nor more representative of the Founders' consensus on these difficult questions, nor, to come to the main point, is there a more reliable guide to civility and citizenship in the American founding, than the words and deeds of General and later President George Washington. Although I have no desire to out-parson Parson Weems, I do think it is impossible to understand the founding without coming to grips with the phenomenon of Washington, which is above all a moral phenomenon of the utmost gravity. In what follows, therefore, I will appeal primarily to his speeches and writings to illustrate my argument.[3]

Civility is in the first place a matter of moral education, involving the shaping of young people's character. The tools of this art include precepts, examples, exhortation, and shame liberally applied as the case permits or demands. It is not surprising, then, to find that one of the earliest writings of the young Washington, laboriously entered into his copybook, is a set of 110 "Rules of Civility and Decent Behavior in Company and Conversation." For the most part these comprehend a lesson useful and necessary for reducing any adolescent to a civilized state: "Shake not the head, feet or legs; roll not the eyes; lift not one eyebrow higher than the other, wry not the mouth and bedew no man's face with your spittle by [approaching too near] him [when] you speak." These rules are a playful (though serious) reminder that civility consists first of all in good manners. "Every action done in company," reads the first rule, "ought to be with some sigh of respect to those that are present." [All citations of Washington appearing in the text refer to W.B. Allen, ed., *George Washington: A Collection* (Indianapolis: Liberty Classics, 1988), hereinafter *GW*. See *GW*, 6.] Of course, bad manners are not evil *per se*, but they can make one unwelcome, uncouth, and in the end unhappy. Good manners are a reminder that one's own interest and happiness are bound up with one's family and friends, and that the authority of such essential social groups is—practically speaking—more obvious than (and just as fundamental as) the liberty of their members.

Civility in this sense stands athwart the contemporary ethic of self-expression. Nevertheless, good manners aim not to crush but to form individual character. Washington's list begins with what might be dismissed today (in theory, though rarely in practice) as mere social conformity; but it ends with these two words: "Labor to keep alive in your breast that little sparkle of celestial fire called conscience" (*GW*, 13). A certain conformity to social custom is part of good manners, but it is justified because we are political animals and because it frees us to cultivate the distinctions that matter. A serious man does not show his seriousness or his superiority by wearing his tennis shoes with a tuxedo or by eating spaghetti with his fingers (though serious men in previous ages have, of course, eaten without forks). Civility allows for, and at its best is, a kind of gentlemanship, the fanning and feeding of that "spark of celestial fire" in man to produce a steady blaze of moral seriousness.

Washington's civility is thus a species of honor or of concern with honor. Explaining to his wife why he had to accept command of the Continental army, for example, he wrote: "It was utterly out of my power to refuse this appointment, without exposing my character to such censures, as would have reflected dishonor upon myself, and given pain to my friends. This, I am sure, could not and ought not to be pleasing to you and must have lessened me considerably in my own esteem" (*GW*, 41; cf. 57-58, 65, 83). As a true gentleman, Washington set high standards for himself; and the consciousness of his own honor, reflected in and reflecting the honorableness of his friends, provided the touchstone of his conduct. At the highest level, his civility was thus a form of magnanimity. Such greatness of soul, as Aristotle explained, accepts external honors as the highest tribute that can be paid it, but regards all such popular offerings as vastly inferior to its own sense of dignity and propriety.[4]

One of the most famous, and instructive, displays of Washington's magnanimity was his response to Colonel Lewis Nicola's letter (May 22, 1782) proposing that Washington be made king. "With a mixture of great surprise and astonishment I have read with attention the Sentiments you have submitted to my perusal," he answered Nicola, a loyal and respected officer.

...I am much at loss to conceive what part of my conduct could have given encouragement to an address which to me seems big with the greatest mischiefs that can befall my Country. If I am not deceived in the knowledge of myself, you could not have found a person to whom your schemes are more disagreeable...Let me conjure you then, if you have regard for your country, concern for yourself or posterity, or respect for me, to banish these thoughts from your Mind and never communicate, as from yourself or anyone else, a sentiment of the like nature. (*GW*, 203-204).

What is remarkable here is the letter's tone—not outraged or accusatory but profoundly surprised and disappointed. It was calculated to shame, not to condemn, and Nicola was so ashamed that he wrote three apologies in as many days. In this short missive Washington refused the honor of being king on the ground that it was beneath him! Honor without principle would be infamy; true honor lay in performing just and noble deeds for their own sake, not for the sake of any extrinsic and unworthy rewards. And in the most fundamental sense of the word, the letter's tone was "civil," that is, it was not the voice of a commander upbraiding his inferior officer, but of one gentleman remonstrating with another, one *civilian* to another. The foundation of civilian control of the military was the civility of the commanding general—the perfect gentleman's civil or reasonable control of his militant passions.[5]

Thus did Washington's civility lay the basis and set the standard for republican citizenship in America. In a way, the crowning glory of the Founding may therefore be said to be the fact that Washington was unanimously elected America's first president. His virtues may be considered the final cause of the new regime, even as they played an indispensable role in its efficient causation, the victories won by the Continental army. Be that as it may, the formal cause of the new order was something different. This was the great principle proclaimed in the Declaration of Independence, "that all men are created equal." It is a matter of some academic and political dispute how this was understood at the time. Certainly, however, there should not be any dispute over how Washington understood it.

As over against those present-day commentators who emphasize the lowness of "unalienable rights," reducing them to expressions of the most elemental passions, to the desperate liberty of doing anything to appease one's fear of violent death, Washington esteemed them as high and dignified principles. Far from signifying the abandonment of virtue, man's natural rights required the virtues to sustain and justify them. As he put it in his general orders to the army on March 1, 1778, the fortitude of

> the virtuous officers and soldiery of this Army...not only under the common hardships incident to a military life, but also under the additional sufferings to which the peculiar situation of these States have exposed them, clearly proves them worthy of the enviable privilege [*sic*] of contending for the rights of human nature, the freedom and independence of their country. (*GW*, 95; cf. 220, 222, 237).

These rights were not antipolitical or directed against the political spiritedness of gentlemen. On the contrary, as Washington noted when explaining (in 1774) his opposition to the British government's policies, it was "an innate spirit of freedom" that first told him "that the measures, which the administration hath for some time been, and now are most violently pursuing, are repugnant to every principle of natural justice." He went on to say that "much abler heads than my own" had fully convinced him not only of the measures' repugnance "to natural right," but of their subversion "of the laws and Constitution of Great Britain itself" (*GW*, 38). "Abler heads" were needed not so much to describe natural justice as to expound the positive law of Great Britain: natural right was in harmony with the spiritedness of his own soul.

In addition to Washington's own "sacred honor," then, there is an honor due to human nature, which honor may be called the right of man. It is an "enviable privilege" to contend for them because they are something special, that is, they are based on what is special to man—his rank in creation. The human species is implicitly distinguished from other species, man from non-man. Man's possession of reason distinguishes him from the beasts, but his imperfect possession of reason—that his faculties are fallible, and above all that his passions may cloud his reason—distinguishes him from the being or the kind of being whose rationality is perfect and unaffected by desire. Non-man includes, therefore, not only the subhuman but also the superhuman, the idea of the divine nature. As the in-between being, man's dignity derives from his place in this ordered universe; it does not result from the attempt to make himself the master and possessor of nature.

The rights of man are governed by man's nature, which means man's place in nature, which means the natural law. For man to deserve his rights, he must live up to the law that ordains them: he must be and act like a man to deserve the rights of man. Writing to the inhabitants of Canada, Washington contrasted "the Blessings of Liberty" with "the Wretchedness of Slavery," warning the Canadians that to submit slavishly to Great Britain would show their "poverty of Soul and baseness of Spirit." Instead, he called upon them to prove "that you are enlightened, generous, and Virtuous; that you will not renounce your own Rights, or serve as Instruments to deprive your Fellow subjects of theirs" (*GW*, 47). Today, unalienable rights are often presented as being a repudiation of the high-minded concern for moral virtue; they are depicted as part of the Hobbesian attempt to demoralize political life. But in the original American understanding, the rights of man are so far from being demoralizing that they in fact demand an unprecedented moralization (properly so called) of politics.

To grasp the significance of this for American citizenship, it is important to understand the relation between what the Founders called civil and religious liberty. Indeed, Washington expressed the whole purpose of the Revolution in those words: "The establishment of Civil and Religious Liberty was the motive which induced me to the Field..." (*GW*, 271).[6] This motive takes us to the heart of the problem—the theological political problem, as Spinoza called it—confronting the Founders.

In the ancient world, this problem did not exist because there was no divorce between the gods and the city. On the contrary every city had its own gods and understood itself either to have been founded by these gods or to have been founded by mortals who were later taken up into heaven as gods (voluntarily or not: Romulus's promotion was said to have been the handiwork of assassins sent by the Senate).[7] The "constitutional" law of every ancient city was therefore divine law. Consider the opening question of Plato's *Laws*, the Athenian Stranger speaking to the Cretan and the Spartan: "A god, is it, or some human being, who is credited with laying down your laws?" The Cretan responds (on behalf of the Spartan, too) "A god, stranger, a god."[8] Or consider the children of Israel, who, except for their monotheism, were a typical ancient people. They were emancipated, conducted out of Egypt, given their law, and led into battle to secure the Promised Land, all by their God.

The ancient city as such had no "religion." It had only its gods, law-giving gods, who were perforce jealous gods. To be sure, some cities held some gods in common, most notably the Olympian deities among the Greek cities, which is why, incidentally, the Greeks could hold the Olympic games. But these gods commanded different things to different *poleis*, and at any rate were only part of the elaborate structure of local and ancestral gods that cumulatively distinguished each city. (Fustel de Coulanges has given the clearest picture of this in his classic book on the ancient city.[9]) The city was the work of its gods, who in return demanded not so much faith, or belief in particular doctrines, but obedience to the city's laws. Indeed, if the city was defeated in battle, its gods were also considered losers; and it was not thought craven or impious for the vanquished (if their lives were spared) to transfer their allegiance to the gods of their conquerors.

When Christianity conquered Rome, however, the nature of political life and citizenship in the West was profoundly changed. Rome had already destroyed the independent civic life of its rival *poleis*, but now the last and greatest of the ancient cities was itself cut off from its gods. In their place rose the Christian God, One and separate from the created world, knowable only through His revelations, the God of all men everywhere but of no city in particular. Now it was that the idea of "religion" was born, for men's civic and divine loyalties were no longer identical. However various the cities of men, the City of God was one. The children of Israel, like every ancient people, had believed itself to be the city of God or of the gods. Under the Christian dispensation, however, the City of God was not a human or earthly municipality. Divine law was no longer constitutive of particular polities, but offered the means of salvation to individual souls in every city. Hence the problem: If the principle of civic obligation was obedience to the divine law, and cities were no longer thought to have divine lawgivers, what principle was to oblige citizens to obedience? How were the various cities and their laws to be justified?

If the whole world were Rome, then the problem might be mitigated or dodged by identifying that city with the city of God—the ancient city writ large. But citizenship in the far-flung Roman empire was more a legal formality than a share in political rule; and at any rate, a single political community, even for the corner of the earth conquered by Rome, proved unsustainable. The political history of the West after the establishment of the Holy Roman Empire consisted of a series of attempts to answer these fundamental questions—to find a new ground for political right. Each attempt ultimately unravelled, partly because Christians fell to fighting among themselves over the exact definition of Christianity, but more profoundly because of the conflict between revelation as such and reason. This conflict underlay the battles between theological and secular authorities during the Holy Roman Empire and during and after the Reformation.[10]

In the face of this theological-political problem, citizenship and civility were both endangered. As a religion not so much of law but of belief, Christianity, when established by temporal authorities, had the distressing if somewhat paradoxical tendency both to sap obedience to civil laws and to invite civil coercion in matters of faith. By virtue of the first tendency, citizenship became peculiarly problematic. By virtue of the second, civility and gentlemanship became swamped by fanaticism and hypocrisy. For gentlemen, according to Aristotle, are precisely those who do not need extrinsic reasons to be moral; they act for the sake of the virtues themselves, guided by practical wisdom. As a political phenomenon, as a real force within the city, gentlemanship is only possible where religion is civilized, i.e., friendly to morality and the rule of gentlemanly virtues.

Restoring the foundations of gentlemanship, civility, and citizenship within the Christian West was the great accomplishment of the American Founding. It did this in the name of civil and religious liberty, not of virtue *eo nomine*, for the deepest cause of the civil war within the West might be said to be the dispute over the ultimate or transpolitical meaning of virtue—whether it consisted in following Athens or Jerusalem, in skeptical questioning or faithful obedience. But this was a debate that had precisely to be carried on at the highest intellectual and spiritual levels. As a theoretical question, it called for conversation among friends disposed to seek the truth. It could not be conducted politically, and any attempt to decide it politically was bound to be ignorant, presumptuous, and finally tyrannical. This had been the cause of the holocausts of the Old World. In America, men would have the liberty to carry on this transpolitical conversation while cultivating the civic and religious friendship that was its precondition and product.

Two principles were therefore required: a ground of citizenship and a ground for separating citizenship from church membership or religious belief. Both were found in the doctrine of natural rights or the rights of man. In the first place, the basis of political obligation was found in the consent of each individual, premised on the grounds of his natural freedom and equality. This individualism had to be as thorough-going as Christian individualism—recall the affecting scene of Christian's departure from his family and village in *Pilgrim's Progress*—in order to establish a common and unshakable foundation on which to build a doctrine of civil authority. The decision to form a civil society thus involves the particular exercise of rights that are prescribed by the universal "laws of nature and of nature's God," eliminating any conflict between the particular and the universal. At the same time, religious liberty is secured by virtue of the limited nature of the social contract. Freedom of the mind cannot be alienated, so that it is impossible to grant to government the power or right to compel our minds to believe something of which they are not persuaded by the evidence and arguments presented to them. Especially is this true of religious questions, for faith above all cannot be forced or extorted.

By virtue of these principles, men may be good citizens of the City of God and good citizens of their particular earthly cities without prejudice to either. "Civil government" and "civil liberties" are made possible precisely by excluding questions of revealed truth from determination of political majorities. Majority rule and minority rights can be made consistent only on this basis. Under modern conditions, limited government is thus essential to the rule of law. But the justice of limited or moderate government for all times and places depends upon a higher, indeed the highest consideration, namely, the limits of human knowledge, whether viewed in the merely human or Socratic light, on the one hand, or the light of divine omniscience on the other. In particular, for the Christian West, the separation of church and state means that revelation is not forced to overrule the protests of human reason, nor reason compelled to pass judgment on the claims of revelation. The limits of human wisdom from every point of view thus affirm the justice of limited government and of citizenship governed by civility.

Although church and state must be separated, this is not true for religion and politics more generally, or for religion and morality, which are distinguishable but, politically speaking, inseparable. Today, the separation of church and state is often regarded as the beginning of the divorce between morals and politics or between values and facts. What this interpretation overlooks is the fact that separation was intended not to separate but to unite civic morality and the *moral* teaching of religion: disestablishment was meant to *establish* common standards of morality to guide political life. The point is well illustrated in the Founders' use of the term "conscience." In general, conscience is the knowledge of right and wrong that men share with one another and with their Creator. It comprises the duties men owe to their Creator, especially the duty of worshipping Him according to the modes we think He finds agreeable—hence the "right of conscience." Writing in 1789 to a group of Quakers, Washington expressed the idea in these words:

> The liberty enjoyed by the people of these States, of worshipping Almighty God agreeably to their consciences, is not only among the choicest of their *blessings*, but also of their *rights*. (*GW*, 533)

That is, religious freedom is not only a dispensation of a loving God who abhors persecution, but also of the fallible human reason that admits it cannot penetrate the highest mysteries of faith.

But conscience comprises also the duties men owe more particularly to themselves and to other human beings. Yet the Founders distinguished the commands of conscience in this sphere from the "right" of conscience grounded in the limits of human reason. Our duties to our fellow man depend not upon a right to interpret private or revealed wisdom but upon our duty to acknowledge the "self-evident" truths of human nature, the special status of man in the universe, whether that universe is thought to be ordered by the inherent power of nature or by the will of the Living God. In short, because human knowledge of the highest things is limited does not mean that we know nothing at all, that we cannot tell the difference between a man and a pig. Such fundamental distinctions must be knowable if revelation itself is to make sense—in order to know, e.g., that "love thy neighbor as thyself" applies to neighboring human beings but not cows or horses. The broad morality built on the commonsense of revelation and reason—on "the laws of nature and of nature's God," properly so called—was what the Founders meant to inculcate as America's public orthodoxy.

One of Washington's most famous letters, composed during his first term as president, is to the Hebrew Congregation in Newport. All Americans, he writes,

> possess alike the liberty of conscience and immunities of citizenship. It is now no more that toleration is spoken of as if it were the indulgence of one class of people that another enjoyed the exercise of their inherent natural rights, for, happily, the Government of the United States, which gives to bigotry no sanctions, to persecution no assistance, requires only that they who live under its protection should demean themselves as good citizens in giving it on all occasions their effectual support. (*GW*, 548)

Good citizenship involves more than simply a *quid pro quo* for the state's protection, however. It requires that those whose citizenship depends on the rights of man conduct themselves as *men*. In other words, to be worthy of the rights of self-government they must show themselves capable of governing their own passion, of governing themselves. Despite reason and revelation's disagreements about what is trans-moral—where nature or God is the highest principle—they agree substantially on the definition of morality. The moral virtues provide a touchstone to help distinguish good from bad citizenship, and true from false prophecy. As Washington puts it in a letter to the General Assembly of Presbyterian Churches:

> While all men within our territories are protected in worshipping the deity according to the dictates of their consciences; it is rationally to be expected from them in return that they will be emulous of evincing the sanctity of their professions by the innocence of their own lives and the beneficence of their actions; for no man, who is profligate in his morals, or a bad member of the civil community, can possibly be a true Christian, or a credit to his own religious society (*GW*, 533).

Washington's point is that the "right of conscience" cannot command anything contrary to the natural law. The right of conscience itself being one of man's natural rights, it has to be exercised consistently with the rest of them. The same point may be expressed in religious terms: new revelations cannot repeal or contradict the basic moral commandments of the Bible.

It is common in the Founders' writings to come across the distinction between public and private happiness. The innermost core of the distinction is the profoundly private relationship between the individual soul and its Creator. The blessings of this communion have in them an element utterly transcending the worldly realm of citizenship, inasmuch as they involve the destiny of the individual soul in the life to come. Within this world, however, public and private happiness are aspects of the same reality. Above all, both public and private happiness are connected to moral virtue. "The foundation of our national policy," Washington urged in his First Inaugural Speech, should be "laid in the pure and immutable principles of private morality" (*GW*, 462). In his Farewell Address he proclaimed, "Of all the dispositions and habits which lead to political prosperity, Religion and morality are indispensable supports. In vain would that man claim the tribute of Patriotism, who should labor to subvert these great Pillars of human happiness, these firmest props of the duties of Men and citizens." Religion and morality are not merely means to political prosperity, it should be emphasized. They are "these great Pillars of human happiness." Happiness is a condition or activity requiring morality and religion; without them, one cannot be genuinely happy, although he concedes that "the influence of refined education on minds of peculiar structure" may in a very few cases allow morality alone to suffice (*GW*, 521).

In his First Inaugural, Washington had emphasized the same point: "...[T]here is no truth more thoroughly established," he declared, "than that there exists an indissoluble union between virtue and happiness..." (*GW*, 462). Morality, or morality and religion, were therefore indispensably necessary to the happiness of the American people. Accordingly, the line dividing church and state or private and public did not run, as John Locke had seemed to argue, between the soul and the body.[11] It ran *within the soul*, distinguishing the exercise of the right of conscience, with its concern for the suprarational doctrines of revealed religion, from the consciousness of moral right.[12] The political effects were striking. With the doctrines of speculative theology now free to be expounded and contested in the churches, uncontaminated by the secular pursuit of power, morality and the moral teachings of religion were free to wield an unprecedented influence over public and private opinion. This *moralization* of politics gave an unprecedented scope for gentlemanship and civility—for what might justly be called Christian gentlemanship.[13]

It was the statesmanship of the Founders, and above all of Washington, that secured this realm of gentlemanly civility for the United States. "We are a young nation and have a character to establish," Washington wrote candidly in 1783 (*GW*, 246). The founding properly so called was nothing other than this great act of establishing the American character. To do justice to Washington's role would require a biography, not an essay; but the core of his genius was always to recognize the moral implications and consequences of human action. He knew when and how to conciliate opinions—on the democratic character of the House of Representatives (the subject of his sole intervention in the debates of the Constitutional Convention), on the Bill of Rights, even among party factions in his own cabinet—so that his countrymen might join hands as fellow citizens. Most importantly, he knew the power of his own example. During the ratification debates he wrote confidently of the historic role that the first officers elected under the Constitution would be called upon to play.

> I have no doubt but...those persons who are chosen to administer it will have wisdom enough to discern the influence which their example as rulers and legislators may have on the body of the people, and will have virtue enough to pursue that line of conduct which will most conduce to the happiness of Country; as the first transaction of a nation, like those of an individual upon his first entrance into life, make the deepest impression, and are to form the leading traits in his character.... (*GW*, 387)

The means and ends of founding are the great themes of classical political science. This science is indispensable to the proper understanding of the American Founding, despite the fact that it was not an ancient city Washington and his allies were establishing. The United States might be a new Rome, but it would not be the old Rome or a mere imitation of the old. Ancient Rome, it suffices to say, would never have described its reason for being as "protecting the rights of human nature and establishing an Asylum for the poor and oppressed of all nations and religions" (*GW*, p. 237). But this did form a great part of America's purpose. In the Founders' view, American citizenship and civility were distinguished by their dedication to the common purpose of Western civilization.

Neither the best city of the classics nor the holy city of the church was what the Founders sought, but a policy that for the first time in history would seek to do justice to both without establishing either at the expense of the other. This was the *novus ordo seclorum* they proclaimed.

To Washington belongs perhaps the most striking statement of the Founders' consciousness of the West as a civilization. It occurs in his famous Circular Letter of June 14, 1783, and deserves to be quoted in full.

> The foundation of our empire was not laid in the gloomy age of Ignorance and Superstition, but at an Epocha in which the rights of mankind were better understood and more clearly defined, than at any former period; the researches of the human mind, after social happiness, have been carried to a great extent; the Treasures of knowledge, acquired through a long succession of years, by the labours of Philosophers, Sages and Legislatures, are laid open for our use, and their collected wisdom may be happily applied in the Establishment of our forms of Government; the free cultivation of Letters, the unbounded extension of Commerce, the progressive refinement of manners, the growing liberality of sentiment, and above all, the pure and benign light of Revelation, have had a meliorating influence on mankind and increased the blessings of Society. At this auspicious period, the United States came into being as a Nation, and if their Citizens should not be completely free and happy, the fault will be entirely (*sic*) their own. (*GW*, 240-41)

The auspices could not be more favorable, but the political lesson is that the freedom and happiness of the American people, and the destiny of the civilization they represent, depend on their conduct. "This is the time of their political probation," Washington adds in the next paragraph, "...the moment to establish or ruin their national Character forever...." (*GW*, 241).

The civility of the American founding connects the American citizenship to the civilization of which it is an illustrious part, but a part nonetheless. One might say that this civility looks to the other part of the civilized world as a kind of community of like-minded nations. Thus the Declaration of Independence pays "a decent respect to the opinions of mankind," presupposing that those opinions are at least decent enough to merit respect. But Washington and the signers of the Declaration were well aware that "cruelty and perfidy scarcely paralleled in the most barbarous ages" could be committed by "the Head of a civilized nation"—

were aware more generally that ages of science and commerce could be as barbarous, in some respect more barbarous, than ages of "Ignorance and Superstition."

It was precisely such a threat from within that faced the United States less than 75 years later in the Civil War, when civility and citizenship were rent in two by the controversy over slavery. It was in the midst of this crisis that Abraham Lincoln, leaving Springfield for the nation's capital, declared somberly that he went "with a task before me greater than which rested upon Washington." In contemplating the future of American citizenship and civility, in contemplating the future of the West, we ought to remember how he bore the task—and what he may have learned to help him bear it, as an avid young reader of Parson Weems's *Life of Washington*.

NOTES

1. Aristotle, *Nicomachean Ethics* 1155a23-28.
2. Aristotle, *Politics* 1272b25-1273b26, 1293b14-18.
3. In fairness to Parson Weems, his biography of Washington has not been read lately with the political sophistication it deserves. For the beginning of a correction, see Garry Wills, *Cincinnatus: George Washington and the Enlightenment* (Garden City, N.Y.: Doubleday, 1984), chs. 3-4.
4. Aristotle, *Nicomachean Ethics* 1123b17-1124a19.
5. Consider this passage from Gouverneur Morris's eulogy to Washington:

> Heaven, in giving him the higher qualities of the soul, had given also the tumultuous passions which accompany greatness, and frequently tarnish its lustre. With them was his first contest, and his first victory was over himself. So great was the empire he had acquired there that calmness of manner and conduct distinguished him through life. Yet those who have seen him strongly moved will bear witness that his wrath was terrible. They have seen, boiling in his bosom, passion almost too mighty for man; yet when just bursting into act, that strong passion was controlled by his stronger mind. Having thus a perfect command of himself, he could rely on the full exertion of his powers, in whatever direction he might order them to act.... Hence it was that he beheld not only the affairs that were passing around him, but those also in which he was personally engaged, with the coolness of an unconcerned spectator.

As Morris remarks, "None was great in his presence." *Eulogies and Orations on the Life and Death of General Washington* (Boston, 1800), 44-45, quoted in Wills, *Cincinnatus,* xxiii-xxiv.

6. Cf. his letter of November 16, 1782, to the Reformed Protestant Dutch Church in Kingston: "Convinced that our Religious Liberties were as essential as our Civil, my endeavors have never been wanting to encourage and promote the one, while I have been contending for the other...." *The Writings of George Washington,* ed. John C. Fitzpatrick, 39 volumes (Washington, 1931-44), vol. 25, 346-347.

7. Cf. Cicero, *De Re Publica* I.25, II. 17-20.

8. Plato, *Laws* 624a.

9. Fustel de Coulanges, *The Ancient City* (Garden City, NY: Doubleday Anchor, n.d.; orig. pub. 1864).

10. See the important discussion in Harry V. Jaffa, "Equality, Liberty, Wisdom, Morality, and Consent in the Idea of Political Freedom," *Interpretation,* vol. 15, no. 1 (January 1987), 24-28.

11. John Locke, *A Letter Concerning Toleration* in *The Works of John Locke,* 10 volumes (London, 1823), vol. 6, 9-13.

12. For a fine account of how this principle was translated into legal and constitutional practice, see Michael W. McConnell, "The Origins and Historical Understanding of Free Exercise of Religion," *Harvard Law Review,* vol. 103, no. 7 (May 1990), 1409-1517.

13. Thus Washington suggested that in America, on the basis of religious freedom, Christianity could achieve a purity and power it had never enjoyed before. "...[T]he consideration that human happiness and moral duty are inseparably connected, will always continue to prompt me to promote the progress of the former, by inculcating the practice of the latter," he wrote to the Protestant Episcopal Church in 1789. He continued:

> On this occasion it would ill become me to conceal the joy I have felt in perceiving the fraternal affection which appears to increase (*sic*) every day among the friends of genuine religion—It affords edifying prospects indeed to see Christians of different denominations dwell together in more charity, and conduct themselves in respect to each other with a more christian-like spirit than ever they have done in any former age, or in any other nation.

In W.W. Abbot, gen. ed., *The Papers of George Washington* (Charlottesville: University Press of Virginia, 1989), Presidential Series, vol. 3, 497.

FIVE

CITIZENSHIP AND CIVILITY AS COMPONENTS OF LIBERAL DEMOCRACY

Clifford Orwin

One hears—and, if you are like me, you acquiesce in—many complaints of the decline of civility in Western society. Civility, however, suggests forms, and forms leave democrats impatient and restless. Yet civility is not just good manners, estimable as those are. Nor is it even law-abidingness, essential as that is. In fact, the devising of civility was identical with that of liberal democracy itself.

Those who lament the passing of civility from contemporary liberal democracy may also variously bemoan the decline of citizenship, of civilization, and of community, all of them somehow related to civility and none identical with it. Let me begin by trying to distinguish between citizenship and civility. Citizenship is as old as the ancient Greek city. It implies membership in a community defined by a common substantive end, more comprehensive, more dignified, more authoritative than the particular ends of private individuals. Citizenship in this sense defines the serious business of life. It supersedes the rest not just because of its urgency but as the proper pursuit of human beings who aspire to nobility and fulfillment. It demands of the citizens great rectitude, great virtues, great dedication, great sacrifices. It therefore supposes unwavering dedication to the ways that constitute a particular community, and requires the strict education and laws which alone foster such dedication. The citizen conceives himself as first of all a part of the greater whole of the city. He is a Roman first, Lucius or Marcus second. He is an individual, with his own needs, interests, concerns, affections, only to the extent compatible with citizenship in the full and primary sense, and so only to a very limited degree.

Civility is the virtue not of the citizen but of a certain version of what Rousseau calls the *bourgeois*. Forget the later Marxian connotations of this term; what Rousseau meant by it was a man living in society who was not a citizen, who was not primarily a part of a greater whole. Such a man is dependent on society without being devoted to it and is dependent on the other *bourgeois* for the satisfaction of both his needs and his self-esteem, while remaining in competition with them for the satisfaction of these same needs. (As Rousseau uses the term *bourgeois* it is simply the alternative to *citoyen* for the man who lives in civil society.) Unlike Rousseau and his followers on the Left, I do not use *bourgeois* pejoratively. One type of *bourgeois*, barely dreamed of by Rousseau but chronicled in a fashion true to his insights by his great student Tocqueville, is liberal democratic man. He represents something less than a citizen, but something more than Rousseau would have expected from the *bourgeois*. His primary concerns are private, but his relations with his fellows are not guided by the mere egoism varnished by deceitful politeness which Rousseau ascribed to the *bourgeois*. His moral compass is civility, a genuine respect for the rights and dignity of his fellow which he conceives with a kind of awe as sacred and equal to his own. Civility too comprises a community, if one far looser than that defined by classical citizenship. It is a community of beings each of whom goes his own way, while recognizing the right of each of the others to do the same, and the common interest of all in maintaining and defending that right.

I know of no text so useful for clarifying the distinction between citizenship and civility as Pericles' Funeral Oration in Thucydides (Thucydides, *Peloponnesian War*, Book 2:34-46). Not only is this speech deservedly the most famous of all celebrations of democratic citizenship, but it also happens to contain the best-known celebration in classical literature of what might sound to us like civility. It is just this seeming combination of the praise of civility with that of citizenship which has made this speech a favorite of liberal democrats. In fact, however, the civility of Pericles' vision of Athens is of our rather than his devising—as it must be, given that his true theme is citizenship in the full sense.

Among the things for which Pericles praises Athens is that it is what we would call a remarkably open society. Whereas its arch-rival Sparta depends for its stability on constraint and coercion, Athens encourages the free flowering of human perfection. This perfection encompasses alike the distinctive excellence of the citizen and that of the human being as such. Of greatest relevance to us is that Athens as Pericles presents it is distinguished by its amazing freedom not only in public matters but in private ones.

> The freedom in which we conduct the affairs of the city extends also to private life. There, far from keeping watch over each other, we do not begrudge our neighbor's acting as he pleases, nor do we afflict one another with those looks as painful as any legal penalty. (2:37)

According to Pericles, censoriousness is unknown at Athens. Both law and opinion permit the Athenian to go about his own life unhindered. It is tempting to conclude from this that Athens celebrates diversity, and that (as with "multicultural" Canada today) this celebration of diversity is what defines its unity. It is tempting but it would be wrong.

For the Athens of the Funeral Oration is unambiguously one in which citizenship takes precedence over civility, in which the diversity of the society (and the value placed on diversity) is trivial in comparison with the demands of citizenship considered as an overarching unity. Decisive is that in Pericles' scheme everyone is a citizen first, held to a very high standard, that of participation in a whole the greatness of which dwarfs the parts. To put it another way, tolerance of diversity (while a fine thing and a rare one) comes cheap at Athens because it is confined to private life, which is much less significant than public life. When off duty the Athenian may act as he pleases, but it is on duty that he shows himself an Athenian. His private pleasures are merely a respite from public cares (2:38); as for his private cares what distinguishes the Athenian is that he never permits these to distract him from public ones. Private life is a stumbling block in the way of civic virtue, and Athenians should be relentless in their disapproval of stumblers. The one thing that Athenians explicitly do not tolerate, according to Pericles, is men immersed in private life. "To mind one's own business" is actually a reproach at Athens (2:40.1; cf. 53.2).

To use words that are not Pericles' but which are useful to us in understanding him, the meaning of life at Athens must be sought in the public sphere rather than in the private one. One's true life is one's civic, not one's civil life. In this all citizens of Athens are alike, although theirs is the sameness of human perfection rather than of the anonymous mass. The Athenian seeks above all to be remembered, to fashion a glorious marmoreal image of himself to be revered by all posterity, and though he craves remembrance as an individual, he can gain it only as an individual *Athenian*, as one hero among many. The lofty communion to which Pericles summons the citizens is one of resplendent self-sacrifice—only by giving themselves wholly to the city can they hope to find themselves, those glorious selves to which they aspire (2:42-43). The diversity of the citizens is superficial; it is admirable only because it is superficial. It is a tribute to the nobility of the Athenian that his private life can be so much his own and his soul remain so much the city's (2:39).

For the opposing view in antiquity, according to which true humanity is more a private than a public matter, we must turn to philosophy or comedy. Consider such plays of Aristophanes as the *Acharnians,* the *Birds,* and the *Peace.* Each boasts a protagonist who flaunts his distinctness from his fellow citizens and concerns himself with leading a life of his own—a life of which the city is at best a burdensome condition, and at worst a vindictive enemy. In each play the author placates the city by presenting this life of self-indulgence as both shameless and preposterous (as resting on stratagems the impossibility of which is hilarious), and so as no less comic than the civic life which is thus evaded. Only the ridiculous is never subversive, since who blames it as such can only appear ridiculous himself.

I have opposed civic to civil, but we must begin from the crucial historical fact that for liberalism the primary opposition was between civil and ecclesiastic or divine. (Such is the sense of civil in, for example, Locke's *Treatise on Civil Government,* in implied opposition to the theocratic politics of Filmer, and in Rousseau's chapter "Of the Civil Religion," the alternative to which is priestly religion.) The civil so conceived included that sphere of life that we would describe as civic (although from the very beginning liberalism stressed the civil at the expense of the civic). This opposition between ecclesiastic and civil was one that liberalism found and so did not have to invent, but its re-interpretation of which defined it as liberalism. Liberalism did not have to invent this opposition because it was the inevitable outcome of the triumph of Christianity in the West and the consequent division of human life between spiritual and temporal, or otherworldly and this-worldly spheres. This division had, in the considered understanding of all the greatest early modern thinkers, destroyed forever (or for as long as Christianity lasted) the possibility of citizenship in its original or full-blooded sense. Under Christianity the unity that such citizenship presupposed was simply an impossibility. The existence of an independent priesthood for whom rulership was an anomaly because it served a prince whose kingdom was not of this world necessarily implied the distinction of spiritual and temporal, ecclesiastical and civil. I quote Rousseau:

> What the pagans feared happened. Then everything took on a different appearance, the humble Christians changed their language, and soon this supposedly otherworldly kingdom was seen to become, under a visible leader, the most violent despotism in this world. However, since there has always been a prince and civil laws, this double power has resulted in a perpetual conflict of jurisdiction that has made any good policy impossible in Christian States, and no people has ever been able to figure out whom it was obligated to obey, the master or the priest.

A few paragraphs further on:

> Of all Christian authors, the philosopher Hobbes is the only one who correctly saw the evil and the remedy, who dared to propose the reunification of the two heads of the eagle, and the complete return to political unity, without which no State or government will ever be well constituted. But he ought to have seen that the dominating spirit of Christianity was incompatible with his system and that the interest of the priest would always be stronger than that of the State.

The division between church and state had thus sealed the fate of human beings not as members of a single community which subsumed and superseded all others but as subjects of a plurality of claims, none of which was simply comprehensive but the boundaries of which were ill-defined. It had divided men within themselves, as none could ever be sure to whom he owed allegiance concerning what. It had also divided them among themselves, as they disagreed on the issue just stated as well as on the crucial question of which of the inevitable plurality of contenders for spiritual authority was the legitimate one. Diversity rather than unity now dominated political life, and with it perpetual discord. Medieval political thought was one long effort to resolve the tension between spiritual and temporal, inclining now to one side, now to the other. Modern political thought offered a more drastic remedy. It sought to solve the problem by abolishing it, thereby inaugurating the reign of civility.

Civility represents the point at which the classical and Christian traditions of Western politics, so long at tension, were finally induced to converge—a convergence which depended, however, on profound modifications of both and which fell far short of a synthesis. Civility represents, in other words, the distinctive liberal transformation of, and sole approved liberal heir to, citizenship and Christian charity alike.

Civility marks so great a sea-change in matters of both politics and religion that it is now difficult for us to grasp the pre-modern character of either. A modern Christian is precisely one who accepts the correctness of civility as an interpretation of the requirements of charity. He agrees, in other words, that charity requires that we refrain from coercion in matters of faith, that all such coercion is downright un-Christian. His pre-modern brethren, of whatever sect, were virtually unanimous that charity demanded that we exert coercion in matters of faith. For salvation being by faith, which was to say by the true faith only, one was obliged to do as much as one could to propagate the true faith and to uproot false ones. This naturally included the proscription and punishment of false teaching, the chastisement of obdurate heretics, and the vigorous persuasion of tepid ones. It was the duty of every Christian monarch to promote the true faith, and so of every kingdom to be of the true faith; conversely, one could not possibly be bound to obedience to a heretical ruler in matters touching on faith. Yet for reasons already stated, every ruler was compelled to legislate in matters touching on faith. In the absence of agreement on the true faith, agreement which by the seventeenth century had become conspicuous by its absence, there was no chance of peaceful relations either between nations or among subjects or between subjects and their rulers.

Against this background civility emerged and assumed its distinctive character. We can best describe that character not as non-Christian but post-Christian. The inventors of civility aimed to break the political hold of Christianity without giving mortal offense to moderate or persuadable Christians. They therefore presented civility not as rejection but as transformation of Christianity. They tricked it out as the true interpretation of Scripture, which had eluded the intolerant sects. It was for this reason that the classics of civility took the form of Scriptural commentary, like Spinoza's *Theologico-Political Treatise* and Locke's *Letter on Toleration* and *Reasonableness of Christianity as Delivered in Scripture.*

Civility or "toleration" (as they called it) was the means by which its founders sought to reconcile the requirements of civil tranquility with the existence of rival Christian sects. The classic solution to this problem was Locke's. It drew a sharp distinction between the respective spheres of church and state, and forbade each from meddling in the other. Although Locke himself described this solution as "toleration," the term, precisely because it was not new, was somewhat deceptive. It seemed to imply that even under the new dispensation a state's sectarian minorities would exist at the sufferance of a majority. In fact under Locke's scheme there was to be, officially speaking, neither majority nor minority. For the state was of no religion, and so in no position to "tolerate" citizens of some other religion. All were equal in its eyes so long as they subscribed loyally to its purposes, and its purposes were in no way religious. (The clearest and most beautiful statement of the misleadingness of the term "toleration" is that of George Washington in his letter of 1790 to the Hebrew Congregation of Newport, Rhode Island. Blunter and less gracious is Jefferson's remark in his *Notes on the State of Virginia* that "[whether my neighbor says] there are twenty gods, or no God...neither picks my pocket nor breaks my leg.") The state aimed not to save souls, but only to protect life, liberty, and property.

Not that religion in the citizens was not useful or even necessary to the state. Spinoza, Locke, and almost all who followed them (the American Founders, for example) insisted it was. But only that religion was useful which had made its peace with the secular state. As the state was of no religion, so it respected no religious authority as superior to its own, in matters which fell within its legitimate purview. The state had the right to legislate in all matters related to the secular welfare of the citizens, and its word was law for them, religious considerations notwithstanding. Moreover, the secular authority, and no religious one, was the legitimate judge of what fell within the purview of secular authority. And as the state was of no religion, no religion could cloak itself in the state's authority so as to coerce other religions. The theorists of toleration attacked the notion of a Christian commonwealth because so long as the state was deemed to serve Christian purposes, it was inevitable both that sects would fight over it and that each would reject its authority whenever it was not within their control. So while Locke and his followers wisely presented toleration as a means of getting the state off the back of the churches, their chief concern was very clearly to get the churches off the back of the state.

The intention of toleration as a grand political strategy may be reasonably construed as anti-Christian. At the very least it clearly proposed to expel Christianity from public life. Christians, however, were not slow to acquiesce in it. For one thing the various sects, exhausted by two centuries of strife, were willing to renounce their claims to political primacy provided that their rivals did the same. For another, Christianity peculiarly lent itself to radical reinterpretation on this issue of church and state. More otherworldly than either Judaism or Islam, it proposed a sharper distinction between the things of this world and the things of the other, and deprecated more than its rivals did the temporal in favor of the spiritual, as well as law in favor of faith and charity. Ironically, the very dismissal of civil authority as merely temporal authority (which had justified medieval thinkers in subjecting it to the spiritual authority) offered modern thinkers the entering wedge for banishing religion from politics. Hobbes, Spinoza, and Locke all insisted that by justice and charity the Gospel meant, above all, law-abidingness, respect for the civil rights of one's fellows, and abstention from coercion or persecution in matters of faith. They insisted, in other words, that the core of true Christian charity was liberal tolerance of rival Christian sects and even of the presence of non-Christian sects—so long as these sects were themselves tolerant. In effect the very practice of tolerance—the rejection of the notion of Christian politics—vouched for the presence of Christian faith. Conversely, insistence on a Christian commonwealth whose purpose was the salvation of its citizens—and which, inevitably, must prove sectarian and therefore intolerant—was held the worst of crimes against charity. True Christianity required support of a commonwealth in which Christianity took a back seat, of a state which was utterly indifferent to Christianity except as nondenominational means to its merely secular ends. Paradoxical and implausible as this ultimately was and is as an interpretation of Christianity, it was plausible enough to gain wide credit among those who wanted to believe it. In the long run all modern Christians have wanted to believe it—in fact that, as I have already suggested, is what has made them modern Christians.

Civility was also the new virtue which was largely to take the place of citizenship in the new post-Christian society. Citizenship in the strong or classical sense was of course long dead, but one might in principle have attempted to revive it (Machiavelli had dreamed of doing so). In fact, however, for many of the same reasons that civility was preferred to sectarianism, so was it preferred to citizenship.

No one would deny, I think, that citizenship in the liberal republic is but a shadow of its preliberal self. Yes, the liberal democratic citizen is capable of patriotism and, where necessary, sacrifice, and yes, the primacy of the civic reasserts itself even in liberal democracies at moments of intense controversy or crisis. Only tyrants have been such fools as to underestimate liberal citizens whose backs were to the wall. Liberal societies, however, naturally shrink from such crises, even postponing them to their peril. In such societies, as Hegel argued, civil society preoccupies the citizens in peacetime, and the public and its call to civic nobility resound only in times of war. Hegel (and Churchill, who appears to have held similar views) had reason to fear the atrophy of citizenship in liberal regimes. For peace rather than war is certainly their normal state, the proof of which could not be clearer. There has never been a war between two liberal democracies. Their lifeblood is not war but commerce. In foreign affairs the classical republics typically aimed at acquiring glory by subjecting their neighbors; the modern republic aims only at avoiding being subjected by its neighbors. It is as reluctant to rule others (except when it can persuade itself that it does so only to liberalize or emancipate them) as it is determined to rule itself. Liberalism and empire do not mix—as confirmed by the fate of all attempts to mix them.

In domestic affairs too, politics is kept in its place. The demands made upon the citizen by indirect or representative self-government, in which the people confines itself to choosing those who make the decisions for the society, are incomparably less than those of direct self-government, where the citizens make those decisions themselves. Such indeed was, in the minds of its founders, a great point in favor of representative democracy; that unlike earlier democracies, all of them directly self-governing and all pathetic or resplendent failures, its demands on the people were reasonable. It did not require citizenship in the full, perennially unsuccessful sense. In this too it fostered civility, with which the tumultuousness of direct democracy had never yet walked hand in hand. (In practice, not even the private relations of the Athenians were the hotbed of good feeling praised by Pericles.)

Even more fundamental than the reforms just mentioned was liberalism's insistence that citizens learn to agree to disagree on the question of the meaning of life. Here the liberal critique of classical politics resembled its critique of the priestly variety. The new program relied on the view that the end of politics was the avoidance of the evils attendant upon disagreement concerning the ultimate good rather than the realization of that good—about which nothing could be agreed except that it inevitably provoked bitter disagreement. So long as politics aimed at what was simply best for human beings, whether in this world or the next, it could not hope to avoid what was worst for him in this one: clashing claims to rule, discord and tumult, want and exploitation. What was needed then was a new politics which would turn its back on the best to devote itself to the eradication of the worst, of anarchy, poverty, and oppression. Thus was the renunciation of citizenship in the old sense, of a community united in quest of the best and noblest for man, necessary to the emergence of civility.

What we mean by "civility," then—at least if we speak with that precision which alone renders such terms useful—is not a quality common to a vast range of societies or to all of these in their prime or to all high civilizations, but one which is specific to liberal democracy and is even its presiding genius. I would suggest that in such societies citizenship and civility are related as follows: citizenship largely (and paradoxically) consists in acknowledging the limits of the public realm. What defines liberalism is the substitution in everyday life of civility for citizenship, and so almost a redefinition (practically speaking) of good citizenship as civility. Liberal citizenship (except in times of crisis) may be casual, almost nominal. The full-time job of the liberal democrat is civility. He is neither Roman hero nor Christian zealot. He pays his taxes and he does his civic duty, but surely does not live for doing it.(Indeed it would strike him as an odd suggestion that he live for the performance of his civic duty.) His duties are few and light compared with those of the classical citizen. His life is mostly a private life, and civility mostly a private virtue, the bond uniting honest men busy minding their own affairs.

Civility, then, as contrived dilution of both citizenship and charity, resembles neither friendship nor love nor any sort of intense attachment. It more resembles neighborliness. Good fences do make good neighbors, and in the case of civility these fences are rights. If civility supplies the spirit of liberalism, rights supply the letter. To treat someone civilly means to remain a respectful distance from encroaching on his rights, and to accord him the dignity appropriate to a bearer of equal rights. Civility is one glue of a community of a specific kind, a community of bearers of equal individual rights. It is a form of communitarianism, but it is an alternative to pure communitarianism. We might best understand it as a bounded or differentiated communitarianism. In a healthy liberal democratic society rights would limit the intrusiveness of the community, but a strong sense of responsibility to the community would also restrain the assertion of rights. Civility requires respect for rights, but not every assertion of rights is compatible with civility.

Civic education, accordingly, was to aim primarily at civility, at a habitual respect for the rights of others which would serve to temper one's assertion of one's own. This theme sounds again and again in Spinoza, Locke, and the American Founders, to name merely those thinkers with whom I am most familiar. It is true that, as Burke remarked in *Thoughts on French Affairs*, "the little catechism of the rights of man is soon learned, and the inferences are in the passions." Yet as Burke himself implied, it made some difference that these passions had been revamped as rights. Only then (to cite the context of his formulation) did even illiterate Russian serfs assert themselves as political beings. Yet it was also the case that in this way people clearly came to see the necessity of civility, of respecting in others those rights that they asserted for themselves. While some may read Hobbes, Locke, and liberalism generally as appealing primarily to private interest, I read them as invoking with equal power a novel notion of dignity bound up with the possession of inalienable rights. That it is generally in our interest to invoke those rights is true but by no means exhaustive: our dignity may demand that we invoke them even when our interest counsels silence. The same dignity demands that we respect these rights in others. (On rights and civility see also Professor Robert A. Goldwin's contribution to the present volume.)

I have argued that civility was sharply distinct from both Christian charity and classical citizenship, and was intended to supplant both. In practice, however, theoretically necessary distinctions may get blurred; indeed, their blurring may prove a necessary condition of successful practice. Such has been the case with civility. It is as if centuries of faith and common sense had bequeathed at least to the Protestant West a temporary immunity to those aspects of the modern teaching most dangerous to the very civility which that teaching sought to establish. These aspects were its individualistic, materialistic and atheistic ones. Even, therefore, as the new teaching blunted the edges of Christianity, so residual Christianity blunted the edges of modernity. Such indeed, as already noted, was the clear intention of Spinoza and Locke. They grasped that the success of their project depended not on dissipating the moral impulses of either Christianity or republicanism, but on coopting them. They sought to transform the older traditions from within, thereby harnessing their still abundant energies to the new order.

The theorists of civility sought to incorporate into the new fabric of life not only the traditional restraints and scruples of believers (albeit in a drastically liberalized version), but also many of their traditional hopes and anxieties. Insofar as submission to the restraints of Christianity had been inseparable from sharing in its hopes, something of the religious perspective was preserved in the new civility. The hope of a divine transformation of the world which would put an end to death and our other discontents was succeeded by hopes that the same might be accomplished through human action. This lent to the liberalism proceeding from Enlightenment a certain deep tinge of faith which was earned in one sense (in the sense that the founders of liberalism had carefully cultivated it) but unearned in another—that is, unsupported by the cold reason on which Enlightenment allegedly rested. As for that reason, it was generally content to bide its time. Such Christian fervor as it could not co-opt, it was willing to permit, subject to the qualifications already mentioned—which, for their part, Christians were mostly willing to accept. "Enlightened Christianity" was the order of the day. Christian longings (and indignation) mingled with post- and anti-Christian ones to produce a deeper commitment to liberalism than warranted by merely rational arguments for merely selfish interests.

I know of no more prosaic example but also of no more exquisite statement of this ambivalence than Tocqueville's discussion in the second volume of *Democracy in America* (part 2, chapter 8) of the principle of self-interest rightly understood. This discussion is highly revealing of the assumptions grounding liberal civility. The Americans, as Tocqueville found them, adhered to a doctrine of enlightened self-interest. At the same time they were animated like all peoples by certain moral impulses irreducible to the prospect of foreseeable gain. They were, however, unwilling to own up to any such disinterested inclinations, insisting rather that all good they did was in obedience to the principle of self-interest rightly understood. An American, it seems, would modestly explain that if he had rushed into a burning house to save the children of a stranger, it was because he expected someone to do the same for him sometime. Tocqueville, for his part, doubts not only the truth of the Americans' account of their conduct but also its coherence. He does not regard as "evident in all its parts" the principle so widely and fervently invoked by his American hosts. The Americans presume a reciprocity or justice in human life in the faith that this presumption is rational, yet reason (Tocqueville suggests) cannot establish it.

Tocqueville does not deny (in fact he emphatically affirms) that it is good for a democratic society that its citizens live by this principle. He sees no alternative and regards this one as tolerably effective at maintaining public morality. It is in the interests of society that the citizens pursue a policy not always clearly in their interest as individuals. The Americans thought that by means of self-interest rightly understood they had resolved all tension between the good of the individual and that of society. Their adherence to their calculating principle rested ultimately on an uncalculated hope. When Tocqueville argues in the chapter following that the power of this principle depends finally on its extension to the next world, he indicates that it builds on hopes which reason is incapable of supporting. The principle of self-interest rightly understood, that most prosaic, most utilitarian, most secular of principles, presupposes the existence of a just God.

All of which helps explain why liberalism for at least two centuries managed to command a fervor apparently quite alien to it. Liberalism was less tame when its tinge of residual Christianity was greater, but the excesses to which it tended were less likely to be ones of individualism. In some ways it worked better when it was less perfect, in the sense of less conscious of its implications. Indeed liberal democracy has found itself in the position of the man who having crawled out on a limb has occupied himself with sawing it off. The ongoing dissemination of an ever more radical and comprehensive enlightenment, while it has not produced an informed citizenry, has at least produced a skeptical one. You would have to wear a very peculiar set of blinders not to see that Americans are no longer a Christian people, and that whatever revival is afoot has begun none too soon.

But it is not just that pre-modern traditions are largely non-renewable resources. It is also that neither was ever a wholly reliable prop for civility to begin with. So liberalism suffers with the passage of time from two quite opposite headaches: the decay of the traditions which it sought to co-opt, and their persistence. It has evoked and depended upon certain Christian and civic longings which it has been unable wholly to satisfy. Of course life is nowhere perfect, and it has proved, in the past two centuries, much less imperfect in liberal democracy than elsewhere. Still, as clear-eyed non-utopians who because of the very clearness of their vision saw the necessity of appealing to utopian impulses, the founders of liberalism took a tiger by the tail. They undertook a balancing act of perhaps even greater delicacy than they knew.

They enlisted in their project long-standing hopes for a truly decisive progress in human affairs—for the total abolition of ancient evils. They sketched a future of unimagined peace, prosperity, and goodwill on earth. While they guaranteed public vindication not of happiness but only of the right to the pursuit of it, it was only human to take this for some kind of guarantee of happiness itself. It is not surprising that liberalism was soon succeeded on the Continent by more radical versions of modernity, apparently further from Christianity (and much more thoroughly hostile to it), but more responsive to its immoderate yearnings and more emphatic in promising these an earthly satisfaction. These movements, even where, as in Anglo-Saxon societies, they have not prevailed, have served as the bad conscience of liberalism. They have lured it in expansive directions, towards the making of ever more glimmering promises which, being liberalism, it cannot possibly keep.

The effect of all of which, in the context of our very real social problems, has been to discredit civility and the rights that inform it as mere "bourgeois formalism." While Marx finds few takers these days, this aspect of his critique persists, as often, nowadays, with reference to race or gender as to class. Such rhetoric, even where it supports merely lawsuits rather than lawbreaking, obviously weakens attachment to civility and implies sympathy for those who flout it. It has fostered the rise of the new politics of adversarialism, of a frank insistence on the expansion of the rights of some at the expense of those of others, by way of compensation for past inequities.

Strangely, this surge of individual and group self-assertion draws upon a rhetoric of increased communitarianism—one which also, paradoxically enough, given the link in history and logic between community and homogeneity, seeks to legitimize the widest possible diversity. "Community" and "diversity" converge in such loaded terms of the day as "inclusiveness" (which is deemed to be good) and "marginalization" (which is not). As a radicalization of earlier liberal arguments for tolerance, the rhetoric of inclusion presents itself as just a kinder, gentler stage of the onward march of liberalism.

In fact, however, we must take both the new communitarianism and its liberal pedigree with a grain of salt. One—perhaps the dominant politically relevant—symptom of this rhetoric of inclusion is an open-ended extension of the rights of those deemed "disadvantaged." Rights, too, are nothing new, and their extension to those who lacked them has been a project of liberalism from its inception. Yet the novel emphasis on bypassing the political branches of government in order to seek legal remedies, the insistence that some individuals and groups are entitled to rights to which others are not, the fact that the politics of so-called inclusion so often serves to polarize society, that it issues in demands for public intervention of a scope incompatible with the liberal premise of limited government—all of these are reasons for suspicion. A communitarianism which rests on a debunking of civility as a self-serving contrivance of white Western males is obviously at some remove from the community of attachment to civility which figured in the original liberal intention.

Proponents of the newer tendencies like to call themselves "post-liberal" and even "post-modern"—so we may look forward to the day when they will yield to post-post-liberals and post-post-moderns. For now let's remind them of the basic principle informing (merely liberal and modern) civility—that weak fences (or no fences) make for truculent neighbors. Will adversarialism inaugurate an era of post-liberal good feeling? I live in hope. I do not hold my breath. Mounting litigiousness inside the courtroom; mounting disrespect for law outside it—these are not a recipe for utopia.

An adequate treatment of the impact upon civility of developments in modern thought since Rousseau would have to consider not only his influence but those of Kant, Hegel, romanticism and the German historical school, socialism utopian and "scientific," utilitarianism in English-speaking countries, and pragmatism in America. Some of these have been forces for civility; others have heaped contempt upon it. (One need only mention Marxist critiques of "bourgeois formalism." On hostility to civility among those Western intellectuals who have been its leading beneficiaries one may consult Professor Edward Shils's article in the present volume.) One thing that all of these outlooks have shared, however, those friendly to civility no less than those hostile to it, was a conviction of the obsolescence of its original theoretical basis. In this sense all may be said to have contributed to its progressive debility. Here I will briefly consider the most recent major developments, those flowing from the most radical of great modern thinkers, Nietzsche and Heidegger. These too are far too complicated to be dealt with adequately in just a few words, so I will focus on the one term under which these grave Continental tendencies have been domesticated in North America. That one term is "values," or, in two words, "value relativism."

Value relativism, by proclaiming the impossibility of rational knowledge of what is best for human beings and so of the best political order, consigns all previous arguments for liberal democracy to the museum of outworn misconceptions. The "laws of nature and nature's god" are childish if charming myths, as are the post-Kantian or post-Benthamite arguments for liberalism on the basis of some ground other than nature accessible to reason. This relativism would seem to be radically subversive of confidence in liberal democracy. Most American liberals today still believe, however, as they have for the past two generations, that value relativism fits civility like a glove. Indeed they hold the former to be the indispensable and only reliable theoretical support for the latter, and they attack anyone so rash as to challenge it as an "absolutist" and enemy of liberal democracy. For civility as currently preached entails above all respect for diversity, and value relativism, with its insistence that no "values" can rationally be demonstrated to be better or truer than any other, seems to liberals to vindicate the equality of all ways of life or "lifestyles" that present themselves to be respected. To question relativism, on the other hand, is to open the door to theoretical absolutism and political totalitarianism. (I have been advised by earnest liberals that to pronounce anything better than anything else inevitably leads to fascism in five minutes or less.) These are, quite literally, the most familiar arguments in the world to us: thus do liberals reconcile their political commitments with their intellectual ones.

There are, however, at least two problems here. The first is that there remains that nagging, fundamental, obvious sense in which value relativism undercuts commitment to liberal democracy. Can a relativist really accept liberal democratic values as authoritative? As entitled to prevail over other values? They remain, after all, just one set of values among many. Relativism teaches liberals to tolerate illiberalism. Michael Dukakis was once quoted as denying that we Americans had a right to war on the Sandinistas "just because we happen[ed] not to like their government." While one could offer traditional liberal democratic arguments both for and against such a war, Dukakis was apparently suggesting that our preference for liberal democracy over Leninism was an arbitrary one ("just because we happen to..."). We hear every day of the alleged ethnocentric "imperialism" of Western values, i.e., of the supposition that these are superior to others. The relativism from which liberal democracy allegedly follows like the night the day thus breeds at best lukewarm partisans, and at worst handwringing detractors of it.

An even bigger difficulty is this. Is it even true that any sort of tolerance follows logically from the relativist insight? Does it follow from the relativity or arbitrariness of all values that we must not prefer our own to anybody else's, but must treat all people equally? It may help here to recall that tolerance is not the only moral virtue cherished by contemporary relativists. Consider the Sixties, when university faculties and administrations everywhere bowed to requests of student radicals whom they recognized as their moral superiors. Was it the tolerance of these radicals which so cowed their professors? Not at all. It was their "commitment." In a world where all values are arbitrary, what impresses most is the resolve with which some people stick to theirs. But how is strength of will related to tolerance?

The cult of commitment is related to that of authenticity, a notion originating in Rousseau but reformulated for our time by Heidegger. Heideggerians, serious or pop, despise liberal democracy for breeding people who concern themselves with making money, mowing lawns and extending the sway of technology, cultivating oblivion to their mortality, the only source of genuineness. Viewed from this perspective civility itself is inauthenticity. And why tolerate inauthenticity, or treat civility civilly? Heidegger certainly did not. Authenticity smiles on self-expression or on perpetual affronts to civility, in our time the grosser the more applauded. The least we must conclude from the implications of commitment and authenticity is that value relativism is a many splendored thing. It equally implies two irreconcilable moral stances, tolerance and intransigence.

Yet according to Nietzsche himself, whose opinion must be allowed some weight, only one of these positions was consistent with the basic insight of relativism, and it was not tolerance. He preaches constant struggle to overcome every obstacle in one's path, great politics, the creation of a planetary aristocracy to impose healthy values on decadent races, and if need be to exterminate them, etc. In fact, according to him, tolerance, equality, democracy, liberalism, socialism—all these things follow not from value relativism but from the lingering Christianity which relativism must sweep away. Historically speaking, liberal democracy, as we have already seen, was the product not of value relativism but of an earlier understanding with which relativism is incompatible, while, again historically speaking, the political fruit of Nietzschean relativism was fascism.

Value relativism then simultaneously supports and saps our attachment to civility. Most professors, those pillars of value relativism, stick to civility while the going is easy, and praise themselves loudly for it. When the going gets tough, they support, or excuse, or at least oppose punishing not stands unpopular on campus (for how many professors wish to be unpopular?) but intransigent expressions of popular ones: shouting down Adolfo Calero, that sort of thing. In the case of a truly unpopular stand, they will at most defend to the death your right to say it...until you have actually said it. For they do not hold more firmly to civility than any other absolute—and relativism affords them endless excuses for trimming. (The classic treatment of all these issues is—and will remain for a very long time—Allan Bloom's *The Closing of the American Mind.*)

Not that most ordinary people do not have better sense than professors: of course they do. And, to tell the truth, America has greater problems these days with citizens who have never learned civility—the ones who crowd our penitentiaries and, in even greater numbers, our streets—than with those who have moved on to better things. Still, the dual rhetoric of tolerance or "empathy," on the one hand, and determined self-assertion, on the other, has confused even many ordinary people, and given aid and comfort to many hardened and vicious ones. They surely feed the too great permissiveness of contemporary societies. (On which see Professor James Q. Wilson's article in the present volume.) For this, professors must certainly shoulder their share of the blame (which they will not be reluctant to do, mistaking it as they will for credit). The claim that liberalism is best because no way of life is best, not even liberalism, is a much less firm argument for civility than the original ones. A great challenge facing liberal democracy is the renewal of those original ones.

Civility can seem conservative today. But what its defenders are groping to conserve is liberalism. Although even so-called liberals must routinely invoke "law and order," few of them have their hearts in it. Yet law and order, enforced as much by a spirit of lawfulness as by a good police force, is really just the heart of civility, which is to say of liberalism itself. If liberalism must shun the "L-word," if it can no longer speak its name, that is only because the people at large have the sense to prefer the thing to the word.

SIX

INCIVILITY AND CRIME

James Q. Wilson

Of late, modernization has been accompanied by criminality. Though there are some noteworthy exceptions (Japan being the most prominent), the economic advancement of a nation has been purchased at the price, among other things, of higher levels of property crimes and, to a lesser extent, of violent crime. Yet the evidence is quite clear that those individuals who are most likely to commit crimes are not the most obvious beneficiaries of modernization; the criminals today, like the criminals of yesteryear, tend to be the poor and the unschooled. How can we explain the failure of economic progress to produce higher levels of "law-abidingness," especially since the progress has reduced the relative size of the population most likely to break the law?

This question is the more puzzling when we realize that it is only economic progress in its contemporary form which seems to be associated with increased criminality. In the early nineteenth century, crime and disorder were quite common in the large cities of Europe and the United States; but then it became less so in the second half of that century, even though the size and density of these cities were increasing dramatically. Ted Robert Gurr found that in London, Stockholm, and Sydney, the number of murders, assaults, and thefts that came to the attention of the police declined "irregularly but consistently for half a century or more" (Gurr, 1977:118). Public safety continued to improve in these cities well into the twentieth century. In Boston, Philadelphia, Rochester, Muncie, and New York City, crime rates rose in the early nineteenth century and then began to decline beginning around the middle of that century (Lane, 1979, 1980; Johnson, 1978; Richardson, 1970; Gurr, 1981; Hewitt and Hoover, 1982; Monkkonen, 1981; MacDonald, 1982). Philadelphia is the best studied city in this regard. There, Roger Lane counted 3.3 murder indictments per 100,000 persons in the middle of the nineteenth century but only 2.1 by century's end, a decline of 36 percent (Lane, 1979).

The second half of the nineteenth century was a period of industrialization and urbanization and, in the United States, one in which millions of immigrants entered the nation. Despite rapid economic growth and convulsive social changes, crime rates appear to have declined or, at worst, to have traced an irregular pattern around a relatively stable trend line.

The contemporary period has also been one of economic growth and urbanization, but unlike a century ago these changes have been accompanied by higher rates of crime. In the United States between 1960 and 1978, the robbery rate more than tripled, the auto theft rate more than doubled, and the burglary rate nearly tripled (Hindelang, Gottfredson and Flanagan, 1981:290). Beginning around 1955 the rate of serious, "indictable" offenses in England began increasing at the rate of ten percent per year (McClintock and Avison, 1968:59). Murder rates during the 1960s rose in, among other cities, Amsterdam, Belfast, Colombo, Dublin, Glasgow and Helsinki; the general crime rates rose in, among other countries, Denmark, Finland, Norway, and Sweden (Archer and Gartner, 1980; Gurr, 1980; Davies, 1983).

Crime rates are less in underdeveloped nations than in developed ones, though the rate of crimes against persons is higher in the former than in the latter (Viccia, 1980). This means that as a nation progresses economically, the total crime rate will increase, but the fraction of those crimes that are violent ones will decrease (Wolf, 1971; Wellford, 1974).

One obvious, but partial, explanation for the difference between these two centuries is the age structure of the population. In the second half of the nineteenth century, in both the United States and much of Europe, the proportion of young persons in the population declined as life expectancy increased. During the 1960s and 1970s the proportion of youngsters in the population increased as the baby boom generation came of age.

However, age cannot be the whole story. In Roger Lane's study of Philadelphia, the increase in the median age of that city's residents was not enough to explain the decrease in homicide rates during the nineteenth century (Lane, 1979:60, 71, 153). Scholars who have examined the upsurge in American crime during the 1960s and 1970s have concluded that the shift in age composition explains no more than half the increase and probably less (Sagi and Wellford, 1968; Wilson and Herrnstein, 1985:426; Ferdinand, 1970; Wellford, 1973; Chaiken and Chaiken, 1983; Fox, 1978).

We have quite clear evidence that much of the recent increase in crime is the result of the greater rate at which young people commit crimes. Marvin Wolfgang and his associates in the University of Pennsylvania followed the criminal careers of two groups of boys, those born in Philadelphia in 1945 (and who remained in that city until they were eighteen) and those born in Philadelphia in 1958 (and also remained in that city for at least eighteen years). Though roughly the same percentage (about one third) of each cohort had at least one arrest, the number of arrests of those boys in the second cohort who had committed at least one crime was much higher than was true of the members of the first cohort. The boys who grew up in the 1960s and who had started on a life of crime committed twice as many burglaries, three times as many homicides, and five times as many robberies as the boys who grew up in the 1950s (Wolfgang and Tracy, 1982). To put it in technical language, the age-specific arrest rate (and thus presumably the age-specific crime rate) of the newer cohort was much higher than that of the older cohort. The evidence we have from the nation as a whole confirms the Philadelphia data. The probability that a person age fifteen to 29 would commit a murder in the United States increased by nearly fifty percent between 1955 and 1972 (Archer and Gartner, 1984:143).

Urbanization also tends to increase crime by increasing the frequency with which persons encounter criminal opportunities (goods to be stolen or persons to be assaulted) and criminal associates (gangs and "criminal subcultures" that one can join) and increasing the chances of evading social sanctions by virtue of the anonymity that cities tend to confer. There is no doubt that crime is more common in big cities than in small ones. But Philadelphia was not a bigger city in the 1960s than it had been in the 1950s—in fact, it was smaller—yet, as we have seen, young boys growing up there were more criminal, and more violently criminal, in the 1960s than they had been in the 1950s.

Moreover, in the 1890s over a million Philadelphians went about their daily business in an environment so orderly that a present-day resident of that city who was transported back a century in time could be pardoned for thinking he had entered Arcadia (Lane, 1986: 7, 14). While it is true that New York City, Istanbul, Manila, and Calcutta all experienced increases in the homicide rate as they grew in population during the first half of the twentieth century, Bombay, Helsinki, Tokyo, Madrid, Belfast, and Nairobi had murder rates that declined as their population grew during the same period (Archer and Gartner, 1980; 1984). In the second half of the nineteenth century urbanization was associated with declining crime rates.

Perhaps the economic cycle has affected crime rates in a way that might explain the differences between this century and the last. There is some evidence that in the nineteenth century, property crime increased during periods of recession and decreased during times of affluence (Gatrell and Hadden, 1972; Thomas, 1925). But that connection between economic conditions and criminality no longer seems to exist, or to exist to the same degree (Wolpin, 1978). In the United States, crime rates drifted down between 1933 and 1960 even though the first part of this era included a severe depression (1933-1940) and the second part was one of reasonable prosperity (1941-1960). And the most recent increase in crime (and in age-specific crime rates) occurred during a period of unparalleled prosperity (1960-1980). Even the scholars who find evidence that economic factors have some effect on contemporary crime rates concede that "the major movement in crime rate during the last half century cannot be attributed to the business cycle" (Cook and Zarkin, 1985; see also Wilson and Cook, 1985).

One can perhaps put the matter even more strongly: whereas in the nineteenth century property was linked to the business cycle, today it is not. If true, that represents a profound change in the relationship between human behavior and historical forces. Criminality has been decoupled from economy. If the prototypical novel of crime in the nineteenth century was written by Charles Dickens or Victor Hugo, today it would have to be written by— whom? Someone, I conjecture, attuned to the effect, not of the economy, but of culture. Tom Wolfe comes to mind.

Not having written or read the definitive novel, I offer instead an argument, one that I have advanced before (Wilson, 1983; Wilson and Herrnstein, 1985:416-21, 430-37). It is this: in the mid-nineteenth century, England and America reacted to the consequences of industrialization, urbanization, immigration and affluence by asserting an ethos of self-control, whereas in the late twentieth century they reacted to many of the same forces by asserting an ethos of self-expression. In the former period, big cities were regarded as threats to social well-being that had to be countered by social indoctrination; in the latter period cities were regarded as places where personal freedom could be more secure. The animating source of the ethos of self-control was religion and voluntary associations inspired by religious life, but it was not religion itself that produced the resulting social control; rather, it was the processes of habituation in the family, the schools, the neighborhood and the workplace that produced it. The ethos of self-expression was secular, but it was not secularism itself that led to "excesses" of self-expression; it was the unwillingness of certain elites to support those processes of habituation that, even in the absence of religious commitment, led to temperance, fidelity, moderation, and the acceptance of personal responsibility.

Ted Robert Gurr, following the lead of the German sociologist Norbert Elias, suggested that the nineteenth century witnessed a full flowering of the "civilizing process"—that is the acceptance of an ethos that attached a great importance to the control of self-indulgent impulses (Gurr, 1981; Elias, 1939). Eric Monkkonen said much of the same thing when he observed that from about 1840 into the early decades of the twentieth century, a set of Victorian values acquired a remarkable hegemony in England and America at about the same as the advent of industrialization (Monkkonen, 1981). Martin J. Wiener has argued that this was more than mere coincidence. The British middle class, which had invented industrialization and benefited enormously from it, viewed the resulting economic and urban growth with suspicion and disdain. Educated opinion placed industrialism into a kind of "mental quarantine," elevating in its place a conception of the "English way of life" that glorified the countryside—"ancient, slow-moving, cozy and 'spiritual'." The English character was defined as inherently conservative, and its greatest task lay in "taming and civilizing the dangerous engines of progress it unwittingly unleashed" (Wiener, 1981: ix, 5-6).

Bertrand Russell would later sneer that "the concept of the gentleman was invented by the aristocracy to keep the middle classes in order," but in truth the concept of the gentleman enabled the middle classes to supplant the aristocracy (quoted in Wiener, 1981:13). The landed elite gave way to the industrialists in its own cultural terms: the former ceded power to the latter on condition that the latter become as much like the former as possible.

In the United States there was no aristocracy that the members of the new bourgeois might ape; in its place was evangelical religion. The first few decades of the nineteenth century witnessed serious religious revivals that later became known as the Second Great Awakening. Those revivals involved an intense debate over the meaning of the Bible and how mankind might enter into the right relationship with God. Whatever spiritual effect they may have had, their social effect was enormous. People caught up in them created or joined a host of voluntary associations designed to improve the society by improving the character of its members.

Those associations included temperance societies, anti-slavery movements, Sunday schools, children's aid groups, and the Young Men's Christian Association (YMCA). The reach of these organizations was remarkable. In 1820, fewer than five percent of the adult males in New York City belonged to the lay boards of Protestant organizations; by 1869 this increased to twenty percent and in the latter part of that year, something approaching half of all adult Protestant males in them were members of at least one church-related association. In 1825, the American Sunday School Union claimed that it enrolled one third of all the children in Philadelphia between the ages of six and fifteen. In 1829 over forty percent of all the children in New York City were said to have attended Sunday school. Within ten years of its introduction, the YMCA enrolled more than 25,000 young men.

But it was the temperance movement that had the most far-reaching effects. In the decades leading up to the 1830s, the consumption of alcohol rose sharply. By one estimate, the annual per capita consumption of alcohol was ten gallons in 1829, up from 2.5 gallons in 1790 (Clark, 1976). Respectable Americans were appalled by the result—rowdy urban streets, saloons on every corner, young men showing up for work drunk. In 1829, there was one saloon for every 28 adult males in Rochester, New York, and that city was not atypical (Johnson, 1978).

The temperance movement meant different things to different people. To some it meant moderation, to some total abstinence. Some wanted legal compulsion, others preferred moral suasion. But taken as a whole, the movement embraced almost every stratum of society, including the intelligentsia. By the thousands, men were induced to sign "temperance" pledges, and boys were recruited into the Cadets of Temperance and the Cold Water Army. By 1855, thirteen states passed laws that banned the manufacture and sale of liquor statewide or at the option of cities and counties. The effect of this effort was dramatic. Between 1830 to 1850, annual per capita consumption of alcohol for persons age fifteen or older fell from 7.1 gallons to 1.8 gallons (Rorabaugh, 1979). What effect this had on behavior, especially criminal behavior, is impossible to say, but most people at the time believed that it made differences for the better. And in retrospect we know that the crime rates declined far faster than one would have predicted, knowing only the ages of the population.

Some places were unaffected, of course. The Tenderloin district of New York and other big cities remained riotous, boozy neighborhoods. But social pressures, police enforcement, and the absence of cheap and convenient transportation, kept the rioters and the boozers "in their place," a place that respectable folks rarely visited except on missionary errands.

I suggest that whatever effects these associational activities had, it was as much from the routine moral training and social pressure they produced as from the religious convictions they imparted. I concede that this is pure conjecture since we do not have—and can never have—any measure of either religiosity or habituation. But the conjecture is consistent with what we know about the development of character in people. Aristotle argued that the moral virtues, unlike the intellectual ones, are the product of the regular repetitions of the right actions. We are habituated to temperate and moderate behavior by routinely acting in temperate and moderate ways (*Nichomachean Ethics*, II.1.i). Developmental psychology has confirmed this insight by showing through countless studies how children who are the object of regular, consistent, and appropriate discipline acquire a habitual tendency to control their impulses, take into account the distant consequences of present acts, and attend to the feelings of others (Wilson and Herrnstein, 1985: chap. 8; Kagan, 1984).

Both the public schools and the Sunday schools had a moral object: the production of better children. The object was sought by precept as well as practice, but from everything we now know of child-rearing, practice is more important than precept. In England and in the United States the Sunday schools were staffed by working-class teachers who sought to inculcate values as well as increase literacy. Both were achieved by rote—that is, by the steady repetition of exercises designed to make habitual behavior that otherwise would be episodic, whether the behavior was the recitation of the alphabet and biblical verses, or the observance of the rules of punctuality and good order. By these means, as Thomas W. Laqueur was later to write, "the bourgeois world view triumphed in the nineteenth century largely through consent, not through force." The middle class established a "moral hegemony" (Laqueur, 1976).

Religion played a role in this, but more, I think, as an animating force than as a moralizing precept. Religious sentiments inspired many of these social movements; churches supplied the institutional catalyst for many of these voluntary associations; church-related societies provided the ongoing social reinforcement necessary to sustain participation in the movements and associations. But the associations outlasted their religious inspiration. A spiritual awakening tends to be evanescent, organizations tend to be immortal. The Sunday school, the YMCA, the temperance society—these endured for decades, long after the Great Awakening was but a memory. The Victorians, whether in the United States or England, lived off their capital in more ways than one. They retained "a strong moral consensus long after the decline of the religious faiths that had originally sustained that morality" (Himmelfarb, 1974:298).

What was decisive about the religiously inspired movements of the nineteenth century was that they were endorsed and often led by the upper classes. In this respect, the American experience was like the British one. In both places the "best people" endorsed a view of right conduct and the path to good character that was accepted by almost all classes. Contemporary Marxist historians are correct in asserting that nineteenth-century schools and associations were used to control the working classes. They are also correct in suggesting that the requirements of the industrial workplace rewarded those best able to conform to them and thus encouraged schools to teach those personal traits—order, obedience, punctuality—that would equip people to be successful workers (Lane, 1986:16). They are wrong only in suggesting that this was done only over the opposition, or contrary to the best interests, of those workers. The working classes not only absorbed those lessons and took those jobs, they taught those lessons and sought those jobs.

Today, matters could scarcely be more different. Beginning in the 1920s and resuming (after time out for a depression and a war) in the 1960s, the best people were at pains to distance themselves from, and even to denounce, what their counterparts a century earlier had taken for granted. Religious revivals once led by liberal college students (such as Theodore Weld, a founder of the anti-slavery society) were later scorned by educated persons who saw such enthusiasms as the atavistic rumblings of rural fanatics. Temperance women were disdained as elderly women who wished to bring back prohibition, which "everybody knows" failed. (In fact, it did not fail in one regard: Prohibition did result in reduction of alcohol consumption by at least one-third and perhaps by one-half.) Saloons that were once dens of iniquity were now called cocktail lounges and held to be centers of sophisticated sociability. Cities that were once viewed as the breeding ground of vice and disorder were now hailed as indispensable arenas of personal liberty.

The very phrase "middle-class values" became a term of derision rather than pride. Sigmund Freud was interpreted (wrongly) as having blamed mental disease on the suppression of natural human instincts by artificial social conventions. Margaret Mead became a best-selling anthropologist in large measure on the strength of her claim (now much disputed) that Samoans were happy because they enjoyed greater sexual freedom. Schools were criticized for their emphasis on rote learning and moral instruction and urged instead to foster self-discovery and self-directed learning among their pupils.

These changes in attitude probably affected child-rearing practices, but not much can be said with confidence on this matter. We can observe how people talked about child-rearing; whether what they said mirrored what they did is another matter. In the mid-nineteenth century, mothers were advised by the ladies' magazines of the supreme importance of inculcating moral and religious principles. Corporal punishment even then was subject to criticism, but the goal of obedience was not. In 1890, 1900, and 1910, one-third of the child-rearing articles published in a sample of articles from the *Ladies Home Journal, Women's Home Companion,* and *Good Housekeeping* were about character and development; in 1920, only three percent were (Wolfenstein, 1955; Stendler, 1950). "Personality development" had taken its place.

When parents in Muncie, Indiana, were asked in 1924 what traits they wanted to see most in their children, 45 percent said "strict obedience" and fifty percent said "loyalty to the church." When the same question was put to Muncie parents a half century later, 76 percent gave "independence" as the desired quality and 47 percent said "tolerance." Only seventeen percent now mentioned obedience (Alwin, 1988).

Today, "Victorian morality" and even the era to which the queen gave her name are known to most of us only as a symbol for prudery, hypocrisy, repression, and over-conformity. There were elements of all of these things in nineteenth-century England and America, but there was something else as well—the maintenance of a reasonable degree of social order, without extensive government repression, in the face of massive economic and demographic changes.

Between 1860 and 1960 elite opinion underwent a change, from advocating self-control to endorsing self-expression (or, as it was quickly understood, self-indulgence). Society's fundamental task has always been to socialize its youth, especially during the tumultuous teen years. Never an easy task, it was in the nineteenth century easier than it is today because adolescence—that recognized interregnum between childhood and adulthood—did not exist. As soon as children were physically able to work, they worked, usually on the farm but sometimes in grim, satanic mills and mines. Moreover, there was a cultural consensus about what constituted right conduct, a consensus strong enough to follow and envelop young men and women when they left the farm to work in the growing cities. Today, we live in a world in which the intellectual invention—adolescence—has become a practical reality. Large numbers of young people are expected to be free both of close parental control and the discipline of the market. They live with parents but not under them; they work in the market, but not from necessity. They are free to seek mates, not under the old (parent-defined) rules of courtship but under the new (peer-defined) rules of dating. It is obviously a status both privileged and precarious, one which is well managed only by those young people who have already been set on a proper course by virtue of a sound constitution and responsible parents.

Now what is remarkable about the social invention of adolescence is that, by itself, it led to no very great harm. The vast majority of teenagers grow up to be perfectly ordinary and respectable adults. The reason, I think, is that most parents do a very good job of setting their children on the proper course. A large fraction of the boys (in Philadelphia, London, and Copenhagen, one-third) will be arrested by the police at least once, but the great majority of these will not be arrested again (Wolfgang, *et al.*, 1972; Farrington, Ohlin, and Wilson, 1986:40-41). As Joseph Adelson has reminded us, most adolescents are neither enraged nor disengaged; they are, on the contrary, very much like their parents and usually turn out to be something of which their parents approve (Adelson, 1989).

But the existence of adolescence and a youth culture put some young people deeply at risk, because they have, by virtue of a defective constitution or inadequate parenting, been set on an uncertain or disastrous course. The embarrassment many adults feel at correcting teenagers, the belief inculcated by higher education and the youth culture itself that freedom and self-realization are the supreme goods, the scorn in which Victorian morality is held—all these deprive the at-risk adolescents of the kind of moral instruction the adult world once provided and enforced.

Adolescence by itself is hardly a threatening social invention (Japanese adolescents are not seen as a social problem); the ethos of radical individualism and commitment to self-expression of educated elites is by itself not especially worrisome (nineteenth-century England was filled with the respectable followers of John Stuart Mill). But the two in combination—that is troublesome.

The two coincided in the United States during the 1960s. There ensued a dramatic increase in teenage pathologies—delinquency, drug use, suicide, eating disorders, and teenage pregnancies. The pathologies only afflicted a minority of all adolescents, to be sure, but the minority totalled several million people.

We are not entitled to be surprised. If we set several million teenagers free from direct parental or market supervision, knowing that a fraction of them lack a strong moral compass, or if we expect those young people to learn from what they see and hear around them, and if what they hear is a glorification of the virtues of individualism and self-fulfillment—then we ought to be thankful that there are any adolescents left intact.

In the 1930s, when marijuana first came to public notice, it was routinely condemned by elites who associated it, often wrongly, with Mexican immigrants. Marijuana use did not spread very widely (Musto, 1973). When it reappeared in the 1960s, it was praised as a liberating or at least a legitimate experience and associated with creativity and musicality; its use spread like wildfire. Peyote and other naturally occurring psychedelics were used by Indians for generations, without much notice; when Aldous Huxley, Timothy Leary and Alan Watts, among others, endorsed the consciousness expanding properties of LSD, its use spread rapidly. When cocaine was first introduced in this country, it was thought to be a harmless stimulant, and Coca Cola put it into its soft drink. When elite opinion turned against it, its use shriveled. When cocaine returned to public awareness in the 1970s, it was advertised as being consumed at the best parties attended by the most fashionable people; other people could not wait to try it.

I do not wish to blame widespread drug use on the glitterati; but I do wish to point out that all kinds of ideas—not just Marxism, Keynesianism or capitalism—have consequences. Young people do learn from older people; at-risk young people will learn from the most self-indulgent older people. As Richard Herrnstein has pointed out, morality must be learned just as surely as the multiplication table and the rules of grammar. And like multiplication and grammar, morality is largely learned by rote. That form of learning is now in disrepute, partly because "rote learning" is wrongly seen as the enemy of creativity and individuality and partly because the elites that must inculcate the learning disagree on what is to be inculcated (Herrnstein, 1988).

This change in routinized moral habituation probably affects everyone to some degree, but for most people the effect is minor because their parents and peers have intuitively rewarded decency and punished selfishness and because these people have entered markets and neighborhoods that reinforced the lessons of their early training. But some lack either the earlier training or the later environment, and so become especially vulnerable in the self-indulgent tone of modern elite culture.

Black Americans have been especially vulnerable in this regard. Roger Lane has described how the black homicide rate in Philadelphia rose from the mid- to the late nineteenth century, roughly doubling at a time when, as we have already seen, the overall homicide rates were falling (Lane, 1986:134). Other immigrant groups, notably the Irish and the Italians, had high murder rates when first settling in that city, but very soon their rates began to fall (*Ibid.*, 140-143). Lane attributes the black increase to their systematic exclusion from the economic life of the city, an exclusion that placed the black middle class in a hopeless position: its commitment to respectability was threatened by both whites (who refused to reward respectability with legitimate economic advancement) and by other blacks (who scorned respectability by creating profitable and status-conferring criminal enterprises).

No doubt, exclusion is an important part of the story, but it cannot be the whole story because even sharper increases in black crime rate occurred later, in the 1960s, when the barriers to entry into legitimate occupations were falling rapidly. Adult unemployment rates for blacks and whites were declining when age-adjusted crime rates started increasing. The other part of the story, to which Lane's excellent study offers important support, is that the culture of respectability was itself precarious, such that its reach was limited to a minority of the black minority.

William E. DuBois, the leading black scholar of his time, was himself the exemplar of the respectable Negro: intellectual in his manner, Puritanical in his views, and reformist in his politics. His book about Philadelphia blacks in the 1890s was, at once, the revelation of the extent of racism and segregation and a plea for self-help—based on a strong family life, steady work habits and the strict control of crime (DuBois, 1989; Lane, 1986: 148,155). But the message was not institutionalized or routinized and so did not reach those most in need. The folk culture of urban blacks, as many observers have noted, was and is aggressive, individualistic and admiring of semi-ritualistic insults, sly tricksters and masculine display (Lane, 1986:146; Levine, 1977; Silberman, 1978). This popular culture may have been a reaction against the repressive and emasculating aspect of slavery; whatever its origin, it was not a culture productive of a moral capital which could sustain people facing either adversity or affluence.

The contrast between black, popular culture and that of other repressed minorities—Asian Americans and Hispanic Americans—has often been discussed. This may help explain why, as Lane notes, black crime rates are higher than Hispanic ones, even in cities where black income is significantly higher than Hispanic income (Lane, 1986:4). Glenn Loury (1985) has complained of the continuing failure of the middle-class blacks to provide visible moral leadership on issues such as crime, teenage pregnancy and single parent families. While one can appreciate the desire of black leaders to avoid giving ammunition to racists by publicly discussing the moral decay of some parts of the black community, in the long run silence would be self-destructive.

The question before this panel is whether the sea-change in elite opinion from self-control to self-indulgence was either caused by or will itself undermine liberal democracy. My tentative answer to both questions is "no." There is nothing in democratic theory that leads inevitably to warped elite ethos. Democracy is, after all, only a system for picking rulers. *Liberal* democracy is a more complicated matter, for "liberal" implies that it will be the goal of democratic rule to enhance liberty. But the liberties the better democracies have secured (and on which their perpetuation depends) are the traditional liberties to life, conscience, and property. The United States was fully democratic (except for the denial of the vote to women and blacks) from about the 1830s on. Removing the barriers to female and black participation did not change matters fundamentally; women, especially, voted pretty much as men had always voted. Yet for about a century after the adult white male franchise was universal—after which every office one can imagine was placed under popular control—and after a civil war had began the emancipation of blacks, the United States did not experience, on an age-adjusted basis, a sharp increase in criminality during times of prosperity—until the 1960s.

One may argue that the extension (in my view, the bending) of the constitutionally protected freedom of expression to include not merely political and artistic speech but also pornography and nude dancing has fostered an ethos that harms youthful socialization, but I am not convinced. Scarcely any society consumes more prurient material than does Japan, yet this has not worked any obvious corruption of Japanese character. One might also argue—with, I think, considerably more force—that the multiplication of restrictions on the police has made certain aspects of the culture of self-indulgence, notably drug use, harder to bring under control. That is true up to a point. But it is not yet clear how much would be gained by reducing the constraints on the police. In New York City they made 90,000 drug arrests last year; in Washington, D.C., nearly 13,000; yet only a small fraction of these arrests resulted in a jail term. Whether the fallout is the result chiefly of legal barriers to conviction or a public unwillingness to pay for prison space, I do not know.

If liberal democracy is not to blame, what is? One possible answer is affluence. Only an affluent society can afford an adolescent class; in poorer societies everyone, including the young, must work. Only an affluent society will have a middle class large enough to produce dissidents from the orthodox culture in sufficiently large numbers such that they constitute a critical mass. Only in an affluent society can people afford to buy large quantities of heroin, cocaine, LSD, PCP and crack. Only in an affluent society are there enough consumer goods so that feelings of injustice are sufficiently aroused to lead people to think that they are entitled to everything.

But we have enjoyed affluence before (though never quite on the scale of the last three decades), yet affluence has not before been associated with so great a commitment to hedonism and self-indulgence. The reason, as I have argued, is that in the past, when freedoms were expanded and economic opportunity enhanced in ways that threatened to free young people from the constraints of conventional morality, the defenders of that morality redoubled their efforts to maintain and extend those constraints. Sometimes, as in the Second Great Awakening, it was a religiously inspired effort; but, at other times (perhaps one can place the 1890s in this category), the religious impulse was less important. In the contemporary world, the adult reaction to enhanced adolescent freedom has not been to control the adolescents, but to emulate them. Once upon a time young men waited impatiently until they were old enough to dress like their fathers; today, fathers try to dress like their sons.

What has changed has been the culture. That change can be described as the working out of the logical consequences of the Enlightenment. The Enlightenment meant skepticism and individualism, coupled with the recurring assertion of the possibility of infinite social progress toward perfectibility. This change brought with it extraordinary social benefits—freedom from religious intolerance and sectarian fanaticism, the development of the scientific method and modern technology, and the intellectual foundation for capitalism and thus for affluence. Man was knowable, authority was suspect, society was malleable.

There is no such thing as a free lunch, culturally or economically. The Enlightenment that honored freedom contained within it no principle by which to define the limits of freedom. The skeptical reason that challenged religious, scientific, or political orthodoxy contained within it no principle by which to defend moral orthodoxy. The individualism that unleashed the material accomplishments of capitalism was insensitive to the moral preconditions of capitalism. The Enlightenment has been institutionalized in the university, and there it has become the public philosophy of the millions of people who each year passed through those ivied halls. Fortunately for most of these people, their philosophy does not affect their lives. Having been habituated to goodness by those very processes—adult authority, rote learning, and the maintenance of appearance—that the university teaches them to distrust, they absorb the ethos without changing their habits.

But their public philosophy alters how they define the proper policy for others. It is an "enlightened" philosophy: people should be left alone to do "their own thing"; historical lessons should be subordinated to immediate needs; utility should be maximized but authority distrusted. For two centuries we have been enjoying the benefits of having supplanted revelation with reason. Most of us will continue to enjoy those benefits for centuries to come. But some will know only the costs, costs imposed on them by well-meaning people who want only to do the right thing.

BIBLIOGRAPHY

Adelson, Joseph. 1989. "Drug use and adolescence." Unpub. paper. Department of Psychology, University of Michigan.

Alwin, Duane F. 1988. "From Obedience to Autonomy," *Public Opinion Quarterly* 52:33-52.

Archer, Dane, and Gartner, Rosemary. 1980. "Homicide in 110 Nations: The Development of the Comparative Crime Data File" in *Criminology Review Yearbook,* edited by Egon Bittner and Sheldon L. Messinger. Vol. 2. Beverley Hills, Calif.: Sage Publications.

_____.1984. *Violence and Crime in Cross-National Perspective.* New Haven, Conn.: Yale University Press.

Aristotle. 1941. *Nichomachean Ethics* in *The Basic Works of Aristotle,* edited by Richard McKeon. New York: Random House, 1941.

Chaiken, Jan M., and Chaiken, Marcia R. 1983. "Crime Rates and the Active Criminal" in *Crime and Public Policy,* edited by James Q. Wilson. San Francisco, Calif.: Institute for Contemporary Studies.

Clark, N.H. *Deliver Us From Evil: An Interpretation of American Prohibition.* New York: Norton.

Cook, P.J., and Zarkin, G.A. 1985. Crime and the Business Cycle. *Journal of Legal Studies.* 14:115-128.

Davies, C. 1983. Crime, Bureaucracy and Equality. *Policy Review.* 23:89-105.

DuBois, William E.B. 1899. *The Philadelphia Negro.* Philadelphia: University of Pennsylvania.

Elias, Norbert. 1939. *The Civilizing Process: The History of Manners.* New York: Urizen (reprint edition, 1978).

Farrington, David P.; Ohlin, Lloyd E.; and Wilson, James Q. 1986. *Understanding and Controlling Crime.* New York: Springer-Verlag.

Ferdinand, Theodore N. 1970. "Demographic Shifts and Criminality." *American Journal of Sociology.* 73:84-99.

Fox, James A. 1978. *Forecasting Crime Data.* Lexington, Mass.: D.C. Heath/Lexington Books.

Gatrell, V.A.C., and Hadden, T.B. 1972. "Criminals Statistics and Their Interpretation" in *Nineteenth-Century Society,* edited by E. A. Wrigley. Cambridge: Cambridge University Press.

Gurr, Ted Robert. 1977. "Contemporary Crime in Historical Perspective." *Annals.* 434:114-36.

_____. 1980. "On the History of Violent Crime in Europe and America" in *Criminology Review Yearbook,* edited by Egon Bittner and Sheldon L. Messinger. Vol. 2. Beverley Hills, Calif.: Sage Publications.

_____. 1981. "Historical Trends in Violent Crime: A Critical Review of the Evidence" in *Crime and Justice,* edited by Norval Morris and Michael Tonry. Vol. 3. Chicago: University of Chicago Press.

Herrnstein, Richard J. 1988. The Individual Offender. *Today's Delinquent.* 7:5-37.

Hewitt, J.D. and Hoover, D.W. 1982. "Local Modernization and Crime: The Effects of Modernization on Crime in Middletown, 1845-1910." *Law and Human Behavior.* 6:313-25.

Himmelfarb, Gertrude. 1974. *On Liberty and Liberalism: The Case of John Stuart Mill.* New York: Alfred A. Knopf.

Hindelang, M.J.; Gottfredson, M.R.; and Flanagan, T.J. 1981. *Sourcebook of Criminal Justice Statistics, 1980.* Washington, D.C.: Bureau of Justice Statistics.

Johnson, R.E. 1978. *A Shopkeeper's Millennium: Society and Revivals in Rochester, New York, 1815-1837.* New York: Hill and Wang.

Kagan, Jerome. 1984. *The Nature of the Child.* New York: Basic Books.

Lane, Roger. 1979. *Violent Death in the City: Suicide, Accident, and Murder in 19th Century Philadelphia.* Cambridge, Mass.: Harvard University Press.

_____. 1980. "Urban Policy and Crime in Nineteenth-Century America" in *Crime and Justice,* edited by Norval Morris and Michael Tonry. Vol. 2. Chicago: University of Chicago Press.

_____. 1986. *Roots of Violence in Black Philadelphia, 1860-1900.* Cambridge, Mass.: Harvard University Press.

Laqueur, Thomas W. 1976. *Religion and Respectability: Sunday Schools and Working Class Culture, 1780-1850.* New Haven, Conn.: Yale University Press.

Levine, Lawrence W. 1977. *Black Culture and Black Consciousness: Afro-American Folk Thought from Slavery to Freedom.* New York: Oxford University Press.

Loury, Glenn C. 1985. The Moral Quandary of the Black Community. *Public Interest.* 79:9-22.

McClintock, F.H., and Avison, N.H. 1968. *Crime in England and Wales.* London: Heinemann.

McDonald, L. 1982. Theory and Evidence of Rising Crime in the Nineteenth Century. *British Journal of Sociology.* 33: 404-20.

Monkkonen, Eric H. 1981. A Disorderly People? Urban Order in the Nineteenth and Twentieth Centuries. *Journal of American History.* 68:536-59.

Musto, David F. 1873. *The American Disease: Origins of Narcotics Control.* New Haven, Conn.: Yale University Press.

Richardson, J.F. 1970. *The New York Police, Colonial Times to 1901.* New York: Oxford University Press.

Rorabaugh, W.J. 1979. *The Alcoholic Republic.* New York: Oxford University Press.

Sagi, P.C., and Wellford, C.F. 1968. Age Composition and Patterns of Change in Criminal Statistics. *Journal of Criminal Law, Criminology and Police Science.* 59:29-36.

Silberman, Charles E. 1978. *Criminal Violence, Criminal Justice.* New York: Random House.

Stendler, C.B. 1950. Sixty Years of Child Training Practices. *Journal of Pediatrics.* 36:122-34.

Thomas, D.S. 1925. *Social Aspects of the Business Cycle.* London: George Routledge and Sons.

Viccia, A.D. 1980. World Crime Trends. *International Journal of Offender Therapy.* 24:270-77.

Wellford, Charles F. 1974. Crime and the Dimensions of Nations. *International Journal of Criminology and Penology.* 2:1-10.

Wiener, Martin J. 1981. *English Culture and the Decline of the Industrial Spirit, 1850-1980*. Cambridge: Cambridge University Press.

Wilson, James Q. 1983. *Thinking about Crime*, rev. ed. New York: Basic Books.

Wilson, James Q., and Cook, Phillip J. 1985. "Unemployment and Crime: What is the Connection?" *Public Interest*. 79:3-8.

Wilson, James Q., and Herrnstein, Richard J. 1985. *Crime and Human Nature*. New York: Simon and Schuster.

Wolf, P. 1971. Crime and Development: An International Analysis of Crime Rates. *Scandinavian Studies in Criminology*. 3:107-20.

Wolfenstein, Martha. 1955. "Fun Morality: An Analysis of Recent American Child-training Literature" in *Childhood in Contemporary Cultures*, edited by M. Mead and M. Wolfenstein. Chicago: University of Chicago Press.

Wolfgang, Marvin; Figlio, Robert F.; and Sellin, Theodore. 1972. *Delinquency in a Birth Cohort*. Chicago: University of Chicago Press.

Wolfgang, Marvin, and Tracy, Paul E. 1982. "The 1945 and 1958 Birth Cohorts: A Comparison of the Prevalence, Incidence and Severity of the Delinquent Behavior." Paper presented to the Conference on Public Danger, Dangerous Offenders and the Criminal Justice System. Kennedy School of Government, Harvard University.

Wolpin, Kenneth I. 1978. "An Economic Analysis of Crime and Punishment in England and Wales, 1894-1967." *Journal of Political Economy*. 86:815-40.

SEVEN

THE PROSPECTS OF CIVILITY IN THE THIRD WORLD

Elie Kedourie

The expression Third World began to be current in journalistic and academic discourse from the mid-1950s onwards, that is to say some ten years or so after the end of World War II. The outcome of this war was a revolution in the balance of international forces, and consequently in the concepts necessary to articulate any coherent account of relations between states. Before 1945, when European states were at the center of world affairs, the notions which were found necessary to articulate discourse about international relations were those of the sovereign state, of a Great Power, of the balance of power, of the Concert of Europe, and of empire. After the European civil war of 1939-1945 (which itself was the continuation of the earlier civil war of 1914-1918), the idea of the sovereign state still remained essential to any coherent talk about international politics, but the notion of a Great Power increasingly came to be seen as having little use. Before 1914, and between the two world wars as well, those states which acted as Great Powers and were accepted as such were all European states. The United States, of course, could easily rank as a Great Power, but except for its intervention in 1917-1918, during World War I, it did not pursue what might be called a *Weltpolitik*, and indeed after 1919 withdrew into what is known as isolationism. For different reasons, the USSR, also certainly a Great Power, was not, after 1917, very much to the fore. Its most spectacular intervention in world politics was the pact with Nazi Germany, signed in August 1939, and which heralded, indeed triggered off, World War II.

However, after 1945, it became gradually and increasingly apparent that it no longer made sense to talk of Great Powers. It came to be realized by degrees that the notion of Great Power had to be replaced by that of a superpower, and of superpowers there were only two. In these circumstances, the idea of a Concert of Europe, a Concert directed by the European Great Powers, and the idea of a balance of power—a balance maintained through the changing alliances and alignments of the European Great Powers, became more or less redundant.

Of the European Great Powers, two—Great Britain and France—had large overseas empires, and this indeed was one very important reason why they were Great Powers. Other European Powers—the Netherlands, Belgium, Portugal, Italy, and Spain— also had overseas dependencies, the first three quite substantial ones. All these imperial powers, however, were either ruined by the world war, or considerably diminished in stature. They very soon lost control of their overseas dependencies, in a process which came to be known as decolonization.

The decolonized territories, so called, were endowed with sovereignty and they *ipso facto* became members of the society of states—a society which was a European creation, and the norms of which were articulated by European thinking about international politics and international law.

How, then, were these new states to look upon themselves? Were they simply new additions to the society of states, having the same attributes and the same assumptions about the conduct of international relations as the older, better-established members? After 1918, when new states came into being following the destruction of the Austro-Hungarian and the Ottoman Empires, this seemed to be more or less the case. But a decade or so after 1945, it was becoming increasingly clear that this was no longer to be taken for granted.

A landmark in the articulation of the idea that these new states were something other than simply new members taking their place, in the traditional way, within the society of states was the conference which was held at Bandung in Indonesia in 1955, and which was attended by 29 states. Some of these states—such as

India, Indonesia, and Burma—were indeed newly sovereign. But other states which were there as well, like Egypt or Iraq, had attained independence between the wars. Their presence at Bandung meant that they were effecting a change, possibly far-reaching, in their own self-view.

It is about the time of the Bandung Conference that the idea of a Third World began to be current. The idea was a response to the new reality in international affairs, which was the existence of two dominant superpowers. What the expression Third World meant to convey was that those who were part of it aspired to distinguish themselves from the two superpowers and all those states which had become constrained to be their allies and clients. Many of these states wished to practice what was then called positive neutralism, but later on non-alignment. Would, however, positive neutralism or non-alignment serve as an organizing idea to articulate and clarify this new international phenomenon? Hardly, since the most superficial enquiry would discover that these notions could be no more than labels which covered a great variety of behavior, the real character of which was governed by the interests, the position, the fears and ambitions of each particular state. Almost the only arena in which these notions seemed to have more than a rhetorical significance were the General Assembly of the United Nations and the various UN agencies, where the non-aligned, voting as a bloc, could aspire—for what it was worth—to carry, or to render nugatory, various resolutions, and could thus hope to obtain some shadowy advantage or another in the shadow-play being produced on First Avenue.

That there was, however, a new phenomenon which had to be articulated and theorized by means of a new concept is strikingly illustrated by the fact that a diplomat representing one of the superpowers, the USA, found it useful to operate with a notion similar to that of the Third World, thus indicating his awareness, even before the idea itself became current, that here was a group of states different from those with whom diplomats had hitherto been accustomed to deal. George McGhee served as Assistant Secretary of State for the Near East, South Asia and Africa under President Truman and his Secretary of State Dean Acheson. Giving an account of his activities and experiences in this post in a book of memoirs published in 1983, he very significantly called it

Envoy to the Middle World. The end-papers of the volume are covered by a specially commissioned map which shows the area comprised in this Middle World. As it happens the map indicates that the center of the Middle World is Mecca. McGhee writes that the Middle World

> includes lands stretching on a west-east axis from Morocco and the Pillars of Hercules at the western end of the Mediterranean to the Indian sub-continent and the Bay of Bengal in the East. To the north, the Middle World is bounded by the lands of the Europeans, the Slavs, the Central Asian nomadic peoples and the Chinese. To the south it extends through the waist of Africa and the Indian Ocean; to the east it is bounded by almost impenetrable mountains.... (*The Middle World*, 1)

During the period with which McGhee is concerned in these memoirs—the late 1940s and the early 1950s—large parts of this Middle World were still under imperial rule. McGhee describes the ultimate goal of the policy which he was responsible for executing as "making clear the underlying American sympathy for the aspirations of the colonized peoples for independence," and "encouraging the colonial powers to be more responsive to the needs and demands for progress of the Arab and African populations" (*op. cit.*, 258). Again he declares that the major American objective in Africa was that its peoples should advance in the right direction and in accordance with the principles of the UN Charter. The aim was to favor "the progressive development of the peoples of Africa toward the role of self-government or, where conditions are suitable, toward independence" (*op. cit.*, 129). *Mutatis mutandis*, of course, this policy, thought suitable for Africa and the Arab world, would also be applicable in other parts of the Middle World still under imperial rule. For McGhee, clearly, the Middle World was middle because it was a field of rivalry between the two superpowers, each one of which stood at one end of the middle. The end which this policy envisaged was, McGhee wrote, the creation of a "Free World Community, within which relations between nations will increasingly be governed by mutual respect and accommodation with each other" (*op. cit.*, p. 428).

It is puzzling why McGhee, the State Department and the administration thought that the character of the Middle World was such as to make such a goal in any way achievable. "Mutual respect and accommodation" could not be assumed to reign between states simply because they had the recognized attributes of states. Their rulers rather had to have some idea of the character of the society of states of which they were now members, and some willingness to accommodate themselves to its norms and practices. Such an attitude would, in turn, be intimately related to the ideals of civility current within the states over which they ruled. Neither when McGhee was seeking to apply this policy, nor when he came to write about it, was there any evidence that society and government in the Middle World was such as to allow hope of success. In any case, the idea of a Middle World was quickly overtaken by the similar but rival idea of a Third World—overtaken both in popularity, and in explanatory and persuasive power. The concept of a Third World seemed to bring order to a large number of seemingly disparate phenomena and to set up a political ideal based on this seemingly clear and persuasive analysis—an ideal which, so the analysis led one to believe, could be considered realistic and achievable.

As has been said, at the outset the idea of the Third World generally signified a number of states which did not wish to identify with either superpower, or to belong to the blocs controlled by, or associated with, either. The states identifying themselves as forming a Third World had, most of them, been under imperial rule; they were relatively poor, and mainly suppliers of mineral raw materials or of agricultural produce to markets in the rich industrialized world. The two characteristics which these states had in common were soon conjoined, so that, fairly quickly, the idea of the Third World came to signify states which had recently been under imperial rule, and which were poor because they had been under imperial rule. Very soon after the Bandung Conference this indeed became the prevalent, not to say universally accepted, idea of a Third World. The appellation and that which it signified may have originated about then in Paris. The new, second edition of the *Oxford English Dictionary* attributes first use of the equivalent French expression, i.e., *tiers monde*, to the economist Alfred Sauvy.

It is difficult now to recapture the sense of puzzlement which the expression aroused when it was first becoming current. After some three decades of constant use the puzzlement has gone, and when the words are heard today what more often than not they conjure up is the world which the journalist P. J. O'Rourke describes in his recent book, *Holidays in Hell:*

> Everywhere you go in the world somebody's raping women, expelling ethnic
> Chinese, enslaving stone-age tribesmen, shooting Communists, rounding up
> Jews, kidnapping Americans, setting fire to the Sikhs...and hunting peasants
> from helicopters with automatic weapons. (*Holidays in Hell,* 167)

It is a far cry from McGhee's vision, but also from that of the
institute in Paris devoted to the study of Third World development
which had asked me in 1959 to give some lectures on development
and underdevelopment. It was then that I first became aware of
this concept.

The Third World: why third, one asked. It was explained that
there was a first and a second world, namely the capitalist and the
communist, and then there was the Third World. The explanation,
however, was never crystal-clear or indeed at all satisfactory. It has
become even less so now, when a Fourth World has made its
appearance, consisting of aborigines and other very primitive
groups, said to be the victims of anthropologists' and ethnogra-
phers' insatiable lust for power. The criterion according to which
the first three worlds—but not the fourth—are distinguished is
one which has to do with forms of economic organization and the
possession of the means of production. If such a criterion is being
used, it might make some sense, albeit of a poor abstract kind, to
say that the First World is capitalist and the Second communist.
What, then, is the economic criterion which enables us to identify
a Third World, and distinguish it from the first two? The answer,
however, has to be that we cannot identify a form of economic
organization or of control of the means of production which is
peculiar and exclusive to the Third World.

Can any sense, then, be made of this concept? One would have
to say that if the concept makes sense, this sense must depend on
acceptance of a Marxist schema. In such a schema, capitalists faced
with a diminishing rate of profits at home would have to penetrate
or invade the market of the Third World so that they could obtain
a satisfactory return on their capital. This is the scenario which is
sketched in Volume III of *Capital.* Like so much else in Marx, the
scenario is inspired by, and most probably derives from, Hegel.
One of the most original and powerful notions which Hegel uses
in *The Philosophy of Right* is that of civil society. Civil society, as
Hegel describes it, is in effect the market. In the relevant section
of *The Philosophy of Right*, Hegel brings out and points up the

characteristics of this modern phenomenon and explores the dialectic of industrial production. The process of industrial production becomes powerful, indeed irresistible. So powerful that it bursts the bounds of the home market and, using the oceans as a medium of communication and transport, succeeds in expanding overseas the market for the products of the industrial cornucopia.

A disciple of Marx's, J. A. Hobson, made the connection between the industrial economy and overseas markets heavy with all kinds of sinister consequences. The picture, as he painted it in his book *Imperialism* (1902), is of financiers, mostly Jews, who control the operations of industry and who, in search of larger and larger profits, use their power and influence to manipulate politicians in capitalist countries and somehow induce them to send military expeditions overseas for the purpose of subduing territories from which they will obtain the cheap raw materials they need to keep their factories profitable and so keep on accumulating wealth. This process Hobson called imperialism, thus annexing a word which had previously had a variety of disparate meanings, but which from then on came to have exclusively attached to it the signification with which Hobson endowed it. Lenin's pamphlet of 1916, *Imperialism: The Highest Stage of Capitalism*, is essentially a jazzed-up version of Hobson's work which the Bolsheviks, following their triumph in Russia, spread worldwide.

This account of European expansion overseas, so highly influential that it is now implicitly accepted without question, suffers from a number of serious flaws. The theory, in Hobson's version, applied to Africa and particularly to South Africa. It was indeed the Boer War which had aroused the radical Hobson's indignation and incited him to seek an explanation for what he manifestly believed to constitute unprovoked aggression by a powerful state against a small, weak country striving to preserve its own ethos and way of life against the cupidities and depredations of ruthless foreign adventurers. But if the theory was to be more than indignant rhetoric, it would have to establish a connection between a large number of economic statistics, the reliability of which was anyway open to question, on the one hand, and political decisions taken in London or Capetown on the other—a connection such that the ups and downs in the rate of profit enjoyed by some commercial enterprises correlates with changes in, say, British policy toward the Boer republics. But there was really no evidence which showed a connection between the fluctuation in the profits of the De Beers Corporation and decisions taken by the British high commissioner in Capetown or by the colonial secretary in London. The same was equally true of other military expeditions dispatched by European powers to Africa. In any case, it is quite impossible to differentiate so-called imperialist or colonialist wars from other kinds of wars. The French conquest of Algeria is described as an imperialist war. How different is it, however, from the Arab conquest of Spain or the Ottoman conquest of Greece or the German annexation of Alsace-Lorraine? All wars are, and therefore no wars are, imperialist wars.

The idea that economic expansion overseas is itself a kind of aggression is implicit in the Marxist and Hobsonian doctrine of imperialism. Implicit because in Marxism all economic activity is a zero-sum game: if someone makes a profit, it is because someone else has made a loss. In any economic activity, again, two and only two parties, the exploiters and exploited, confront one another perpetually. No economic transaction therefore can be mutually beneficent. Hence every buyer and seller is a soldier in the class war. Hence also any economic innovation becomes in the hands of its promoters economic aggression. For example, it is contended, following this line of argument, that native Indian textiles and those who gained a livelihood from producing them were ruined by the importation into India of cheap Manchester goods, and that this is clearly economic aggression waged by Western capitalists. Such an argument depends on the assumption that no Indian entrepreneur would have ever, on his own, introduced changes in the manufacture of textiles which would have affected traditional producers in the same way as foreign imports did—in fact, in precisely the same way as cottage industries were destroyed in England by the mechanical loom which made possible the production of cheap Manchester goods. Another assumption also underlies the argument, namely that protectionist measures would have saved native industry, but that the government being British not Indian, it gave preference to the interests of British manufacturers over those of its Indian subjects. What the argument takes for granted is that protectionist measures could not have harmed the interests of the mass of Indians in order to benefit a small group of producers, that a native Indian government would have automatically favored protection, and that the British government of India equally automatically did the bidding of Manchester capitalists. All these propositions may be true, but their truth is not to be derived from a doctrine; it has to be established by evidence.

The doctrine, however, does not seem to have been harmed by paucity of evidence, and recent decades have indeed seen new versions launched and propagated. These new versions are derived from the writings of André Gunder Frank and Immanuel Wallerstein. The picture presented here is of a capitalist world-economy, the mainspring and beneficiary of which is the capitalist industrial system. This system constitutes the center of the world economy, and its very presence inevitably means the perpetual dependence and enfeeblement of the periphery, which has thus to suffer the poverty and powerlessness which goes with dependence. A very recent variant of this line of argument was produced under the auspices of a number of eminences and given wide publicity in the so-called Brandt Report on "international development issues," published in 1980 under the title *North-South: A Programme for Survival.* The distinction on which the report is erected is similar to, if not identical with, the distinction between center and periphery. The North is rich and the South is poor, and the North is rich because the South is, has been made, poor. All these theories, then, have in common an explicit or implicit acceptance of the Marxist schema and Marxist language. It is acceptance of this schema which justified the presence at the Bandung Conference of Communist China, then a member of the Soviet bloc. Its presence was justified on the score that it had been the victim of colonialist aggression and exploitation and was thus a member of what was beginning then to be called the Third World.

The dichotomy North-South, Marxist as it is, yet gives Marxist doctrine a twist which bids fair to make it a heresy. The motive-power which, in Marxism, moves history is the class struggle between the capitalist exploiters who own the means of production and the defenseless working class whose labor—the only commodity they possess—they exploit. In the North-South or center-periphery schema the struggle is not between international capital and a working class whose misfortunes equally transcend national boundaries—a class whose battle hymn is, rightly, the

Internationale. The struggle rather is between the industrialized world as a whole, including both capitalists and workers, and the non-industrial regions whose substance the rich industrial world continually sucks dry. This heresy began to be uttered soon after the triumph of Bolshevism in Russia. Among its proponents were the Russian Tatar, Sultan Galiev, himself a communist, and Li Ta Chao, a founder of the Chinese Communist Party. The doctrine is at the center of the writings of Dr. Frantz Fanon, long accepted by the Algerian FLN as a principal ideologue. President Qaddafi's Third Theory derives indirectly from him. This Marxist heresy opens the way to an amalgam between the two most powerful ideologies of the modern world: Marxism and nationalism. In this amalgam the nationalist struggle against the foreigner is at one and the same time the class struggle against the exploiter.

Such as it is then, the idea of the Third World is built on an economic and political abstraction. For all its power to attract followers and move them to act, the abstraction is a false one: economic activity is not by definition a zero-sum game, governments do not embark on territorial conquest at the bidding of financiers, and there is no simple, clear-cut distinction between northern, exploitative nations and southern, exploited, ones. The concept of a Third World will tell us nothing informative or enlightening about the actual character of the vast regions which are lumped together under the label, Third, or Middle, World with all their enormous differences in history, tradition, geography and economics. The term, in fact, has come to serve as a political weapon, most notably, in order to buttress claims for financial aid from governments of rich countries. This is the stance adopted by the second secretary-general of the United Nations, Dag Hammarskjöld, who preached the necessity of "international justice" requiring the equalization of the economic conditions of all nations. It was also the stance of the so-called Group of 77 at the first UNCTAD (the United Nations Conference on Trade and Development) held in 1964, which demanded the establishment of a New Economic Order through large transfers of wealth from rich to poor countries. Again, hand in hand with the concept of a Third World went, necessarily, the idea of neo-colonialism. Necessarily, because though the government by European states of overseas countries had now disappeared, what did not disappear was the original cause of colonialism, namely the desire by industrial capitalists to exploit the nonindustrial world. Colonialism, therefore, was inevitably succeeded by neo-colonialism, the change from European to native rule being simply a (trifling) change in the superstructure. So long as capitalism existed so would neo-colonialism continue to exist. The idea of a Third World, one may conclude, is tentacular and all-embracing. As such it has to be vague and cloudy, but thus all the more attractive and powerful.

If the idea of a Third World is confused and misleading, can anything which is general be said about the regions which the appellation seeks to embrace? Most, though not all, of them had been dependencies of European states, and as such would have been shaped and influenced by the civilization and political ideas of the metropolitan countries, and the administrative and judicial institutions established by the foreign rulers. In the circumstances, such institutions could not but have been autocratic, but the civil servants who operated them were answerable to governments responsible to parliaments and, to some degree or another, responsive to their own public opinion. Colonial rulers, then, as much in response to their own political traditions as because they were accountable to home governments, established in these territories a *Rechtstaat*, in which judges and courts did not obey the whim of the ruler, and administration operated according to publicly-known rules which were designed to eliminate favoritism and corruption, and to a large extent succeeded in doing so.

Also these colonial administrations, at any rate until fairly late in their history, did not aspire to make comprehensive plans for economy and society. In short they endowed the territories for which they were responsible with a centralized, reasonably efficient and honest administrative structure which, using modern European techniques, allowed the government's writ to run everywhere. When the colonial rulers departed, their native successors inherited this administrative structure which, centralized as it was, could be exploited for different and much more ambitious purposes. The administration was, under the new conditions, free of the checks which accountability to metropolitan governments and legislatures required. Furthermore, those who took over the administration themselves did not operate according to unfamiliar norms inculcated by a long-standing tradition of respect for the rule of law, and by an equally unfamiliar ethic which did not allow private interest to override the requirements of the public service. The heirs of the colonial rulers, in short, had put into their hands a very powerful instrument the use of which was not regulated by the restraints, internal or external, which had earlier existed.

The native political tradition with which the heirs of the European rulers were familiar was either that of tribalism or of Oriental despotism. Particularly in Africa, the logic of tribal loyalties overrode that of the Western-type territorial state. The members of one particular tribe would inherit the colonial administrative structure and possess all the powers of sovereignty which comes with independence. They would thus be able to ride roughshod over other tribes now corralled together within the same state, and would constitute a kind of tribal *nomenklatura*, as East European diplomats serving in Africa have described them. The monopoly of rule by one tribe might however be challenged by the rival tribe or tribes, and the outcome would be either anarchy or simply the transfer of the monopoly of power from the defeated tribe to the one which now had the upper hand. In either case, the rulers lack the legitimacy which comes from the consent or acquiescence of the ruled, and the body politic is bereft of any arrangement for the orderly conveyance of authority from one government to another.

To palliate this lack, governments can now use methods of mass ideological mobilization, unknown to traditional rulers in the past. Such methods have been perfected and widely practiced in Fascist Italy, Nazi Germany, and in the Soviet Union and its dependencies, and would have become familiar to the Westernized native groups who took over from colonial regimes. Such methods would, in the circumstances, have great attraction; they would as well be quite practicable since the governments now control, as a matter of course, the electronic media, the press, as well as school and university education. In brief, highly centralized administration, lack of legitimacy, and an ideological style of politics are the hallmark of government in the tribal societies which European states conquered, governed for a few brief decades and then quickly and suddenly abandoned.

What is true of the tribal societies of Africa and their fate following decolonization, is likewise true, *pari passu*, of those much more sophisticated societies in Asia which, before European rule, had lived under institutions of Oriental despotism. As Karl Wittfogel has shown, Oriental despotism where, as he put it, the state is stronger than society, is the most durable and intricate form of government known to history. In these societies, European rule usually served to temper native despotism, again through the operation of the rule of law and through the accountability of its agents to their metropolitan masters. Also, notably in India, great efforts were made, in the first three decades of this century, to set up institutions of local and provincial self-government. It became clear fairly soon, however, that such institutions had little prospect of taking root and establishing genuinely representative and responsible government. The successful working of such government depends on there being a body of voters not accustomed to passive obedience and able on the other hand to appreciate that the general good can, if only sometimes, have the primacy over private interest. These characteristics being absent, public power remains what it has always been in this tradition, simply the private property of the official power-holders.

As has been said, the concept of a Third World depends on a version of economic history which purports to explain why certain regions remain poor and exploited. The concept, however, is not simply an explanatory device. It is also a doctrine of action. Implicit in it is the demand or the exhortation that the Third World so-called should break the shackles of economic exploitation and attain the level of welfare and prosperity which the exploiters have reached thanks to their unscrupulous exploitation. Hence, as has been seen, Hammarskjöld's demand for global economic equality and the cry for a new world economic order, to be established by means of a vast transfer of wealth from the exploiters to the exploited. Underlying such a demand is the assumption that, given this injection of wealth, Third World governments would be able to make their poor "underdeveloped" countries rich and developed.

This aspiration to economic development, unknown to traditional society but now embraced by the post-colonial rulers, in due course becomes widespread among the Westernized native intellectual and official classes—becomes, so to speak, their particular ideology. However, the very condition of these states—the extreme centralization of government, the insecurity which lack of legitimacy brings, and the ideological style of politics—makes very difficult, or even precludes, the kind of private economic endeavor which brings material prosperity. Centralized economic planning has to be a substitute for the market. The plans, moreover, have to be set up and their execution supervised by the same centralized administration which carries on the usual tasks of government. As experience has repeatedly shown, a centralized administration is unable to cope with this burden. Arbitrariness, inefficiency and waste are the consequence. With them goes a prodigious increase in the official corruption which lack of a civic spirit, and the private appropriation of public power, of necessity entails. The failure of each successive project breeds discontent within the intellectual and official classes and an aspiration to take the place of the power-holders who have failed. Since, in these polities, means are generally lacking for lawful and orderly political change, we see an abundance of military *coups d'état*. The violent shock of the body politic which a *coup d'état* occasions and the stringent precautions which those in power must take in order to preserve their position and their very life will further reduce in these countries the prospects of civility.

EIGHT

CITIZENSHIP AND MIGRATION

IMPLICATIONS FOR LIBERAL DEMOCRACIES

Myron Weiner

For the remainder of this century, and well beyond, liberal democracies will wrestle with the moral and political questions of whether to admit immigrants and refugees, and if so how many, what rights and entitlements they should be given (including the right to stay), whether to grant them citizenship, and if not whether their locally born children should be granted citizenship. These questions arise for two reasons: there is now a greater demand from people from low-income developing countries to enter advanced industrial democracies than the latter are willing or able to admit; and secondly, even when industrial democracies economically benefit from migrants, there is often popular resentment against them. The issues raised are thus largely moral and political, and often only secondarily economic.

Among those countries that share the Western heritage of the Magna Carta, the Bill of Rights, and parliamentary institutions, there has been a convergence on defining the rights of citizens. These rights have evolved from notions of protecting individuals against the state to notions of the state providing individuals with entitlements. Americans, Swedes, French, Germans, Australians, British and Japanese share similar conceptions of citizenship rights largely derived from common liberal democratic principles.

No such convergence exists on the question of who should be admitted to citizenship. Historically immigrant countries such as the United States, Canada, Australia, and New Zealand have welcomed large numbers of immigrants whom they have incorporated as citizens. In contrast most of the countries of Western Europe, which admitted large numbers of migrant workers in the 1960s and 1970s, have been restrictive about the granting of citizenship to the migrants and sometimes even to their locally born children.

While the conception of citizens rights is derived from a common heritage and liberal and social democratic principles, the question of whether immigrants should be admitted, what kind of immigrants, and whether they should be admitted to citizenship is more deeply imbedded in a country's political culture and history.

Countries have five possible options. The first option is not to admit migrants at all and for citizenship to be based primarily on descent. The second option is to admit migrants to fill temporary labor needs, limit their stay and provide only those welfare benefits (such as health care) that are essential to their effective economic performance. The third is to permit migrants to stay indefinitely, grant them many if not all of the entitlements provided to citizens, but exclude them and their children from citizenship. The fourth option is to grant citizenship to the locally born children of migrants, but not to the migrants themselves. And the fifth option is to admit the migrants, as well as their children, into citizenship. Liberal democracies cover almost the entire spectrum, but everywhere the options remain unsettled and the debate over policies and the principles that should underlie policies continues.

WHY THE QUESTIONS MATTER

In the second half of the twentieth century migration to Western Europe, Australia and North America has been largely from the newly independent countries of Asia and Africa, and from Latin America. A high demand for labor in Western Europe in the 1950s and 1960s—the combined result of rapid economic growth and a decline of new entrants into the labor force as a result of low fertility rates and high mortality rates during World War II—led these countries to open their doors to migrant workers from the low-income countries of Southern Europe, North Africa, and Turkey. Though it was expected that the migrant workers would only temporarily reside in Western Europe many migrants brought their families, gave birth to children, and have become permanent residents. In 1990 the number of migrants in Western Europe totalled 12 million: 4.5 million in France, 2.5 million in Britain, 1.8 million in West Germany, nearly 1 million in Switzerland. Most of the migrants are from the Third World: North Africans in France, South Asians in Britain, Turks (and Yugoslavs) in West Germany. While European countries have economically benefitted from the migrants, there is a great deal of hostility to migrants. In France, the hostility is directed toward North Africans, hardly at all to migrants from Portugal and Spain. In Germany, the hostility is toward Turkish migrants, less so toward Yugoslavs. In Switzerland there is widespread popular opposition to what is called "overforeignization." Throughout Western Europe there are now right-wing parties whose central concern is with closing boundaries to new immigrants and forcing existing immigrants to return home. The debate on the continent no longer centers on whether new migration should be permitted (the answer is uniformly no), but whether existing migrants and their children should be admitted to citizenship, to what extent the doors should remain open to refugees, and whether future needs for labor should be met by admitting migrants from among the more easily assimilated peoples of Eastern Europe.

Great Britain was confronted with different issues than those facing other members of the European Community. After World War II, Britain granted citizenship to those who resided within the British Empire and thereafter to the people of those countries who remained in the British Commonwealth. Since citizenship implied the right of abode within Great Britain, many members of the "new" Commonwealth, that is the former colonies of Asia, Africa and the Caribbean, migrated to Britain. As several million migrants from the new Commonwealth entered, the British government was faced with the issue of whether Commonwealth citizenship should include the right of immigration, and whether distinctions on "the right of abode" should be drawn between descendants of British who had settled in the colonies and those who were "native" to the colonies, a distinction with clear racial implications (Peters and Davis, 1986. On British immigration policy also see Layton-Henry, 1985; Ivor Crewe in Glazer and Young; and

Brown in Glazer and Young). More recently, the British have debated the question of how many citizens of Hong Kong (and which ones) who hold British passports (some 3.5 million people out of the five million people residing in Hong Kong) should have the right of abode in Britain.

The United States, traditionally an immigrant country, has been faced with an unprecedented number of illegal migrants, largely from Latin America. The illegal flow was in part a continuation and enlargement of a wartime policy of admitting guest workers from Mexico—"braceros"—to temporarily fill manpower needs in the agricultural industry; but the new flow was largely a response to the growing demand for low-skilled, low-wage laborers in jobs that Americans—including low-income minorities—were unwilling to take. For the United States the policy issue was whether these illegal migrants (and their children) were entitled to any rights and benefits, whether (and how) they should be forced to return home, whether they should be regularized (and ultimately natural-ized), and how future legal flows might be halted.

Japan, a post-war entrant to the category of liberal democracies, was faced with still a different problem. Traditionally not an immi-grant country (notwithstanding a brief history of bringing Korean workers to Japan in the 1930s, many of whom subsequently brought their families and permanently settled in Japan), Japan in the 1980s was confronted with a problem of illegal migration of workers from the Philippines, Indonesia, and Malaysia also responding to the demand by employers for low-skilled, low-wage workers. While the numbers are relatively small, only a few hun-dred thousand, the Japanese are debating the question of whether this ethnically homogeneous country would benefit from import-ing short-term migrant workers and whether migrants should be employed primarily in dirty and dangerous occupations or prefer-ences should be given to those with needed skills (Shimada, 1990). What is not at issue is the question of whether any migrants who are admitted should be granted citizenship, a closed subject to the Japanese.

Australia, a traditional migrant country, historically pursued a "white only" policy, with preference given to those who came from English-speaking Commonwealth countries. Australia was under severe international criticism for its racially restrictive policy, a policy rendered unrealistic by the decline in the number of people from Britain, Canada and other English-speaking advanced industrial countries seeking to emigrate to Australia. Immigration laws were revised, and racial criteria were replaced by considerations of manpower needs and the skills and education of the migrants. The new policy enabled significant numbers of Asians to enter and to become citizens, thereby changing the ethnic composition of a country that had hitherto been culturally and racially homogeneous. In the late 1980s the debate was reopened, with many Australians, concerned with the environmental impact of population growth, calling for a halt to future migration.

These issues—whom to admit and whether migrants should be granted citizenship—have become increasingly important and contentious issues in advanced industrial liberal democracies. The "push" from much of the Third World—where incomes are low, unemployment is high, education is increased but social mobility is limited, and regimes are often repressive—combined with the "pull" from the advanced industrial democracies has created an unprecedented global situation. This has raised two issues. The first is the moral question: do liberal democracies have a moral obligation to admit more people and if so, to anyone seeking a better life or only to refugees fleeing from persecution? If a country does admit immigrants should it do so on a temporary basis, providing short-term employment and income for migrant workers or short-term asylum for refugees, or should it incorporate them as citizens? The second issue is a political one: even if migration and absorption to citizenship is morally desirable and even economically beneficial, is it politically acceptable? Will substantial immigration and the incorporation of migrants into citizenship generate ethnic conflict, stimulate anti-migrant right-wing movements, create a new underclass, and thereby weaken liberal democracies? Before turning to these two issues, we shall first review the approach to immigration and citizenship in several advanced industrial democracies.

CONCEPTIONS OF CITIZENSHIP IN ADVANCED INDUSTRIAL DEMOCRACIES

Citizenship can be acquired in three ways: The most common is by birth, either by place of birth (*jus soli*) or line of descent (*jus sanguinis*). Both conceptions are matters of ascription. Citizenship can also be acquired through naturalization. Naturalization is a privilege. In some societies, however, aliens may claim citizenship as a right upon compliance with the term set by law while in other societies citizenship may be conferred only at the discretion of the state authorities (Plender, 1972).

In the United States individuals become citizens by virtue of having been born in the United States, by birth abroad if parents are citizens, and by naturalization if they comply with the conditions specified by Congress, including five years of permanent residence, understanding the English language, and having a knowledge and understanding of the history and form of government of the United States. The *jus soli* rule has been interpreted by the courts to mean that anyone born in the United States is a citizen at birth, including the native-born children of illegal aliens and short-term visitors (Schuck and Smith, 1985). The Fourteenth Amendment specifies that "all persons born or naturalized in the United States and subject to the jurisdiction thereof, are citizens of the United States and of the state wherein they reside," an amendment which granted citizenship to all Negroes as well as to the children of aliens irrespective of the legal status of their parents.

In 1880 Congress passed legislation excluding from citizenship migrants from China, Japan, Burma, Malaysia, Thailand, Korea, India, the Philippines and portions of the Near and Middle East. The justification for racial tests for citizenship was that certain peoples came from civilizations inimical to the principles of democracy and were incapable of assimilation into the American way of life. The act, in effect, converted Asian migrants into guest workers, permitted to remain and work in the United States, but unable to bring family members. Efforts by several states to further restrict Asian migrants by preventing them from purchasing property were, however, struck down by federal courts on the grounds that such legislation violated the Fourteenth Amendment, which says: "nor shall any state deprive any person of life, liberty or property without due process of law; nor deny to any person within its jurisdiction the equal protection of the laws."

Racial restrictions on naturalization ended more than a half century later, with an act of 1943 which eliminated the ban on the immigration and naturalization of Chinese, a 1946 act which lifted restrictions against Filipinos and East Asians, and the 1952 MacCarran-Walter Act which ended all racial tests for citizenship. The category of aliens ineligible for citizenship was thus abolished (Easterlin, 1982). In 1964 and in subsequent acts Congress abolished national origin quotas for immigration, admitted migrants who satisfied U.S. labor force needs or were rejoining family members, and admitted refugees with a "well-founded fear of persecution." The general thrust of the legislation was to make immigration less ascriptive (exception for family unification) and to facilitate the naturalization of all who entered as immigrants.

In the decade of the 1980s, 5.8 million people were admitted into the United States as legal immigrants. In 1988, 643,000 persons were admitted, the largest legal influx since 1924. Most of the admissions are based upon family relationships without regard to any system of preferences. Others are admitted within a quota of 20,000 persons per year per country. Nearly half of those admitted each year come from Asia (Gordon, 1990). Under the Refugee Act passed in 1980 the United States sets an annual refugee ceiling and allocates that number among the regions of the world. While certain categories of refugees (e.g., asylees, and temporary parolees) are not entitled to federal benefits, most are treated in the same legal fashion as immigrants, that is, they are given permanent legal status which permits them to seek citizenship.

After five years of continuous residence in the United States and passing a test to demonstrate an ability to speak, read, and write English and some knowledge of the U.S. government and history, immigrants can acquire naturalized citizenship. Each year in the 1980s approximately a quarter of a million or more individuals were naturalized. Naturalized citizens have the same rights as native-born Americans with the sole exception that they cannot become President.

The Supreme Court has extended the protection of the Fourteenth Amendment to aliens. The Supreme Court ruled that aliens admitted to legal residence are entitled to most of the benefits of the welfare state (*Graham v. Richardson*, 1971), and that state governments cannot deny employment to aliens for most state civil service jobs (*Sugarman v. Dougall*, 1973), though states can impose restrictions on eligibility when there is a substantial and necessary public purpose (Bennett, 1986). For example state governments can limit employment in the police and as school teachers to citizens. The federal government can also deny resident aliens opportunity for employment in the federal civil service if there is a clear public purpose. Most federally-sponsored social welfare programs, including Aid to Dependent Children, welfare payments, food stamps, old age assistance, aid to the disabled, supplemental security income, and federally-supported housing, are available to resident aliens. Some congressional acts do, however, restrict benefits for aliens (Medicare, for example). Finally, the Immigration Reform and Control Act of 1986 bans discrimination in employment against lawful aliens.

The Supreme Court has also extended certain rights to illegal aliens. The court ruled against a Texas law which sought to deny access to public education to the children of illegal aliens (*Plyler v. Doe*, 1983). Though the children and their parents could be deported, the court said, it was unlikely that they would be. To deny migrant children education would, therefore, create a permanent underclass of migrants. The court, however, was careful not to extend other benefits to illegal aliens, though subsequently a federal judge in New York ruled that undocumented aliens could not be denied Medicaid benefits. It seems inevitable that other cases involving unlawful immigrants will arise. In any event, federal and state agencies rarely check the legal status of aliens, so that illegals often have access to welfare benefits. The courts have also ruled that migrants threatened with deportation are covered by the equal protection clause. The courts have provided some protection for illegal immigrants against unreasonable searches and seizures, though the courts permit the Immigration and Naturalization Service to engage in raids to search for illegals. They have also ruled that unlawful aliens are under the protection of the Fair Labor Standards Act, including minimum wage protection.

The Immigration Reform and Control Act (IRCA) of 1986 offered amnesty to unlawful aliens who had been in the country continuously since December 31, 1981. It is estimated that 2.5 million illegal migrants will be granted temporary legal status under IRCA's amnesty program.

The thrust of congressional legislation, court rulings, and the administrative practices is thus to reduce the differences between the rights and benefits of citizens and of aliens and to extend many rights and benefits to illegal aliens as well. The primary difference between legal resident aliens and citizens is that aliens cannot vote, run for public office, serve on juries and can be denied access to certain public jobs. Deportation of aliens is uncommon, limited largely to convicted criminals. Legal aliens, as we have noted, have virtually the same access to public benefits as citizens; even illegal migrants are entitled to some public benefits, if not legally, then as a practical matter. In short the American practice is to increasingly treat as equals—both with respect to legal rights and social benefits—all who permanently reside in the United States, whether they be native-born Americans, naturalized citizens, legal aliens, or illegal migrants.

The migration and citizenship policies of Europe's democracies and the conceptions that underlie them differ substantially from those of the United States and with one another. They differ both with respect to how citizenship is attributed at birth and how citizenship can be acquired.

In contrast with the American principle of attribution of citizenship at birth based on the principle of *jus soli*, and the notion of legal aliens acquiring citizenship virtually as a matter of right, German citizenship law attributes citizenship at birth exclusively on descent—*jus sanguinis*—and regards naturalization as exceptional. Contemporary citizenship law is based on a citizenship act passed in 1913—known as the Basic Law—which regards descendants of former German citizens as German citizens in the eyes of the Federal Republic of Germany. Moreover, the Federal Republic of Germany did not recognize the division of Germany. Thus, under the Basic Law all East Germans, and millions of ethnic Germans settled in Eastern Europe and the Soviet Union, have a statutory right to enter the Federal Republic of Germany and claim their German citizenship. It is estimated that in 1989-1990 a million East Germans migrated to West Germany.

German citizenship law has deep historical and cultural roots. In the eighteenth and nineteenth centuries when Germany was politically fragmented, Germans developed a sense of nationhood that was independent of the state. German nationality rested upon a linguistic and cultural rather than a political identity. The notion of a single nationality and a single German citizenship persisted even with the partition of Germany and the creation of two

German states after World War II. Thus the East Germans and eth-nic Germans from Poland who fled to the Federal Republic were not regarded as refugees but simply as Germans entitled to move to the FRG and to claim German citizenship.

The Turks, Yugoslavs and Italians who entered Germany as migrant workers were not regarded by Germans as potential citi-zens. Indeed, the Germans frequently reiterated their position that "the Federal Republic of Germany is not and cannot become a country of immigration." Foreign citizens living in Germany, therefore, have no legal right to naturalization and can only be naturalized at the discretion of the German government (Hailbronner, in Brubaker, 1989:67, 68). Naturalization is possible for those who have resided in Germany for ten years, speak German, are committed to the democratic order of the Federal Republic, have a cultural attachment to Germany, and have sur-rendered their emotional and political attachment to their home country. "Political activities in emigrant organizations are usually taken as evidence against a permanent attachment to Germany" (Hailbronner, 69). But even if these requirements are satisfied administrative authorities retain discretion in whether or not to grant citizenship. The result is that few of the 4.5 million foreign immigrants in Germany (7.5 percent of the West German popula-tion) have become naturalized citizens. The immigrants would appear to be permanent: a majority have resided in Germany for more than a decade, and seventy percent of the one million for-eign children under age were born in Germany but are not citi-zens and cannot readily acquire citizenship.

There is, however, one point of convergence between the German and American policies: noncitizens have rights. They are entitled to political rights, including freedom of association, the right of assembly and demonstration, and freedom of speech. Migrants have a right to residence within Germany which entitles them to access equal to that of citizens for employment in the labor market at equal wages. But to discourage further migration, spouses must wait four years after entry before they are eligible to work. The children of migrants have the same rights to education as do German citizens. No distinction is made between citizens and noncitizens with respect to access to social services. Migrants are eligible for unemployment insurance, old age pensions, accident and disability insurance, health benefits, and vocational training on the same terms as German citizens. The primary legal differences between citizens and noncitizens is that the latter cannot vote or stand for public office, are restricted from employment in some public positions, and are exempt from serving in the military.

Israel, like Germany also bases citizenship on descent. Under the 1950 Law of Return, Israel regards all Jews as having the right to enter and settle in Israel. Jewish migrants automatically acquire Israeli citizenship. Arabs who resided in Israel when the state was formed, and children thereafter born to them within Israel, are also citizens of Israel, but Arabs who resided in Israel before independence and subsequently left do not have the right to return. Israeli conceptions of citizenship thus rest on a set of notions about the unity of the Jewish people throughout the world and their claim to a homeland from which they fled into the diaspora. Individuals are Jews by virtue of their descent from a Jewish mother; they need not share a common language or culture, nor do they need to be religious adherents to be regarded as Jewish. Israel thus has two rules of citizenship by birth: those born within the country of parents who are nationals and who are therefore automatically citizens irrespective of religious or ethnic affiliation, and those born abroad who are entitled to immigrate and claim nationality but only if the parents are Jewish.

Countries like Germany, Israel, Switzerland, the Netherlands, and Japan which follow the concept of *jus sanguinis* make naturalization difficult, while those which also subscribe to the notion of *jus soli* tend to be more liberal on questions of citizenship. In the Netherlands, for example, *jus patri* prevails for the children of migrants, and only the third generation obtains citizenship at birth. Migrants can become citizens after five years of residence if the migrant has "a reasonable knowledge of Dutch" and a "sufficient acceptance by Dutch society" (Hammer, 1985:68). But only a thousand migrants are naturalized each year. In Switzerland migrants can be naturalized only by the vote of the communal parliament or in the small communes by an assembly of the citizens, a procedure which keeps the rate of naturalization exceedingly low (Hoffman-Nowotny in Hammer, 1985:222). The locally born children of migrants are subject to the same procedure. (An exception to this generalization is Sweden, which makes naturalization easy though it has a tradition of *jus sanguinis*. See Hammar in Rogers, 1985.)

In France, which subscribes to *jus soli*, locally born children of aliens automatically become French citizens at the age of 18 if they have resided in France for five years and have not been convicted criminals. Children born in France are automatically French citizens at birth if at least one parent was born in "France," inclusive of those born in Algeria and other colonies and territories before their independence. Descent plays a less important role in determining citizenship in France than it does elsewhere in Europe. Brubaker notes, however, that the belief that nationality depends on blood was widely held in France throughout the nineteenth century (Brubaker, 1989:24). It was not until the passage of a new French national law in 1889 that the principles of *jus soli* were adopted. The change was partially dictated by the adoption of conscription, which led many to argue for turning into Frenchmen the one million foreigners (mainly Belgian and Italian) then living in France, of whom 200,000 were males under the age of twenty, and partly by a desire to prevent the emergence of nations within the nation. Republicans believed that foreigners born in France could be assimilated into French life and culture, and that the secular schools and the military were powerful assimilating institutions (Brubaker, 1989, 34).

The post-war migration to France consisted heavily of North Africans, along with Portuguese, Spaniards, and Vietnamese. As elsewhere in Western Europe the migration was regarded as a temporary response to labor shortages and it was widely assumed that the migrants would in time return home. As it became clear that the migrants had come to stay, the response of the French state has been to pursue a policy of inclusion, to provide citizenship to the children of foreigners residing in France, and to admit into citizenship those immigrants who assimilate to the morals and customs of France and demonstrate linguistic competence. Immigrants who had French nationality because they were born in French territories can request "reintegration" into French nationality (Brubaker, 1989:114).

Strong opposition to French immigration and citizenship has come from the National Front, an anti-migrant political party led by M. Le Pen. The National Front has called for the abolition of *jus soli.* In the 1986 elections conservative parties called for legislation which would set conditions for the acquisition of citizenship by the French-born children of foreign nationals residing in France, but the legislation was subsequently withdrawn as a result of popular opposition from parties of the left and an impressive network of religious, student, and human rights organizations. However, whether the children of foreign-born parents should have to request citizenship at maturity is still at issue.

Among the industrial democracies, Australia was the most explicitly restrictive with respect to the ethnic and racial characteristics of those admitted as immigrants and then as citizens. In an effort to increase population Australia promoted large-scale immigration after World War II. The Australian government was committed to maintaining a homogeneous British-like population, but unable to attract enough immigrants from Great Britain the country was opened to continental European immigrants. "We seek to create a homogeneous nation," said an Australian minister of immigration. "Can anyone reasonably object to that? Is not this the elementary right of every government, to decide the composition of the nation? It is the same prerogative as the head of a family exercises as to who is to live in his own house" (quoted by Carens, in Gibney, 45). In 1972 Australia formally ended its White Australia policy with the passage of an immigration law that stated that policy was to be based on the "avoidance of discrimination on any ground of race, color or skin, or nationality" (Carens, in Gibney, 44). The policy shift was in part the result of the pressure upon Australia to end its racial criteria for migration, partly tied to Australia's concern for improving ties with Southeast Asia, and partly a recognition that if immigration was to continue, Asia rather than Great Britain or the European continent was the most likely source (Price, 1973).

Australia grants a full range of civil and social rights to immigrants. The only difference between immigrants and naturalized citizens is that the latter can vote and can hold permanent positions in the public service. Over twenty percent of Australia's population is foreign born, among the highest among advanced industrial democracies except for Israel. Citizenship is easily acquired after three years of residency. Since there are few additional benefits associated with citizenship, migrants who chose to become naturalized are simply identifying themselves with Australia and proclaiming their public allegiance. A recent study reveals that Asian migrants value Australian citizenship more highly than do immigrant Britons: immigrants from the Third World are twice as likely as immigrants from the English-speaking countries to become Australian citizens (Evans, 1987:252). As with other traditional immigrant countries, such as the United States and Canada, Australia regards immigration into the country as tantamount to admission into citizenship.

THE MORAL AND POLITICAL ISSUES

Should borders be open to enable people, irrespective of the accidental circumstances of birth, to move to countries where there are opportunities for a better life? To most people the answer is no, based on the principle of state sovereignty that every state has the moral and legal right to pursue its own national interest even if it means denying entry to peaceful and needy foreigners. It is important, however, to distinguish between two dimensions: admitting people into the country (immigration) and admitting those who are in the country into citizenship (naturalization). The principle of sovereignty addresses the first, but not the second dimension of admission into a state. Nor, it should be added, does the principle of sovereignty necessarily mean that foreigners ought not to be admitted, only that states have the right to determine who and how many should be permitted to enter. A morally concerned people may chose to admit refugees, or to admit people for whom there is a feeling of special affinity, or regard immigration as of national value because the country is in need of skilled manpower, or to seek migrants to do work that local people do not want, or to welcome greater ethnic diversity. But control over entry remains a fundamental right and power of the sovereign state.

The argument against open borders is that unlimited migration would enable a populous country to take over a less populous neighbor, could create massive public disorder as citizens responded to an unwelcome influx, could reduce the economic well-being of some of its citizens (especially those already at the bottom of the labor market), and would of necessity mean the end of the welfare state since the state would be required to render benefits to an unlimited number of people.

Some scholars reject these arguments and call for unlimited migration. Their argument starts with the difference principle in John Rawls' theory of justice, with its notion that under a veil of ignorance individuals would not know into which class or society they would be born into and hence would seek to avoid any disadvantage resulting from birth in a less-favored class or society (Rawls, 1971). Though Rawls himself does not propose that his theory be applied to the international realm with respect to freedom of movement, some of his critics argue that his theories are useful for thinking about questions of justice not only within but across societies. "We can take it as a basic presupposition," writes Joseph Carens, a Canadian political philosopher, "that we should treat all human beings, not just members of our own society, as free and equal moral persons....We should therefore take a global, not a national, view of the original position" (Carens, 1987:256. Also see Carens in Brubaker, 1989, and Carens in Gutmann). In the original position where we operate in a veil of ignorance we would chose the perspective of the alien who wants to be able to immigrate to a more satisfactory location. Would the consequences be riots against migrants? A decline in the economic well-being of the natives? Carens replies that within a society, rioting to prevent others from exercising their rights would not be just, so the argument that unlimited immigration would create public disorder because of antagonistic reactions from current citizens cannot be grounds for exclusion. Moreover, if immigration does reduce the economic well-being of current citizens, restrictions would not be justified if the worse-off (immigrants) improve their lot. "The economic concerns of current citizens are essentially rendered irrelevant" (Carens, 1987:262). Nor is it important to preserve the unity and coherence of a culture if it forces some people to be worse off because they cannot enter into the community. In other words, in a world of open borders current citizens would no longer enjoy a privileged position.

A counter argument has been put forth by Michael Walzer that membership in the community is central to Rawls' theory of justice and hence it does not have universal applicability. Walzer argues that there is a moral distinctiveness to the nation-state, that the state can be regarded as analogous to a private club, and is therefore free to take strangers in or not. (Walzer, 1983:61. On the question of immigration and community, also see Schuck in Glazer, 1985.)

The debate over whether borders should be open is thus also a debate over whether liberal principles of justice are internationally applicable or are restricted to those who live within a liberal democratic society. The critics of the latter position argue that "temporal priority of citizenship does not yield a right to deny this status to others who apply later" (Whelan, 21) simply because some people are born in free and rich countries and others are not. Does a community (in this case, the country-as-a-community) have the right to exclude others from entering their territory when community membership is based upon birth rather than upon consent? Is there a difference between free movement within a country, from one community to another, and free movement of peoples across international boundaries?

Common sense, if not liberal theory, leads one to distinguish between the rights of people to move within a country and rights to international migration. People who are citizens of a political system, by birth or naturalization, are free to move about within their country by virtue of their membership in a national community. But the state—the set of institutions which serves to protect the community—has the right and obligation to protect those who live within its political and territorial boundaries and can therefore regulate who and how many people can enter the territory. On this point, it should be noted, there is no difference between liberal democratic societies and others. Democracies and autocracies share the same belief in the sovereign right to control immigration.

Where there is a difference is in whether the benefits of citizenship—if not citizenship itself—should be given to all who legally reside within the country, including aliens. On this issue western liberal democracies differ from authoritarian states. The United States, Canada, the members of the European Community, Australia, New Zealand, all countries with substantial numbers of immigrants, provide aliens with virtually the same rights and benefits as citizens: access to public education, health care, public housing, unemployment benefits, social security, provision for the disabled, and the full range of political rights, except the rights to vote and hold public office. Indeed, several countries (notably the Scandinavian countries) have extended to legal aliens the right to vote in local elections in order to enable and to encourage migrants to participate in local community affairs which affect their well-being (Brubaker, 1989).

The liberal policy of providing the full range of welfare benefits to immigrants also has the effect of inducing immigrant workers to remain even when there is an economic downturn and a rise in unemployment. The "floor" provided by welfare in the host country is often higher than the income ceiling migrants can expect in their home country, with the result that the various campaigns by European countries to induce migrants to return home have not been successful (Rogers, 1985; and Rogers, 1986).

Societies with authoritarian governments do not usually provide their migrants with the same benefits as citizens. The countries of the Persian Gulf—Saudi Arabia, Kuwait, the United Arab Emirates, Bahrain, Oman, and Qatar—had large immigrant inflows in the 1970s and thereafter as a result of the rise in the price of oil. The massive increase in national wealth led these governments to invest heavily in ports, airports, hotels, refineries, manufacturing plants, housing, roads, hospitals and a variety of other infrastructures. The result was a need for labor not available locally, since each of these countries had small and young populations and social traditions which excluded most women from the labor force. Labor force participation rates were as low as twenty percent. Governments concluded that growth depended upon the importation of a large labor force. The intention was to import labor from Asia as well as from the Middle East, but not to permanently incorporate immigrants into the society. Migrants were granted labor permits to work for specified employers and were not permitted to freely seek employment in the labor market. They were excluded from most social benefits provided to the local population (public housing, health services, and education). They were excluded from buying property or owning businesses. Unskilled migrants were not permitted to bring their families. Workers who broke the law were summarily repatriated. Dismissal by an employer was tantamount to expulsion from the country, so that workers were in no position to protest unsatisfactory working conditions. Notwithstanding these restrictions, millions of migrants, mostly from South Asia, sought employment in the Gulf states. In some Gulf countries the number of migrants exceeded the local population in the labor force.

The aim of preventing permanent migration has been only partially realized. There is a high labor turnover in construction. Workers brought to the Gulf for construction projects are sent home upon the completion of their assignment. But in other sectors of the economy—in industry and in the service sectors—employers seek continuity by regularly renewing their labor contracts. In these sectors the need for migrant labor has persisted in spite of the downturn in the economy. Moreover, many of the more skilled members of the labor force have been permitted to bring their families. The result is that some sectors of the migrant population increasingly have the look of permanency. Migrant communities in the Gulf now have their own temples and churches, restaurants, movie houses, private schools for their children, cultural associations, and newspapers. Many migrants have now spent most of their working lives in the Gulf and their children are staying on. However, it is well understood by the migrants, their families, and their governments, that they do not have the right to remain and that the host government is free to force their departure anytime. Since they cannot own property, savings are sent abroad, often to buy property at home. The migrants regard themselves, and are regarded by nationals, as outsiders, living in but not a part of the host society. They have no attachment to the local culture or to the political system and rarely mix socially with the local inhabitants (Weiner, 1982).

The International Labor Organization has sought agreement to an international convention on the rights of migrant laborers which would assure them of the right to remain, to bring their families, and to share many of the basic welfare benefits provided citizens, but the governments of the Gulf states have rejected these proposals. Their view is that work and even long-term residence within the community does not qualify migrants for membership in the community. They do not accept the democratic principle that there should be equality before the law for all who live within the authority of the state, for these are liberal norms not acceptable to the autocratic regimes of the Gulf.

THE WITHERING AWAY OF CITIZENSHIP?

If within liberal democratic societies citizens and noncitizen migrants share the same rights, of what importance is citizenship?

If all who live within the society are equal under the law, has citizenship ceased to be important? What difference does citizenship make?

Citizenship implies benefits, rights and obligations. Benefits, as we have seen, are with few exceptions equally granted to both citizens and migrants; in the United States many benefits have been extended to illegal migrants as well. Rights too are virtually the same, with two important exceptions: migrants are generally excluded from certain (in some countries, all) public offices, and are nowhere given the right to vote in national elections. Migrants can, however, join public associations or form their own, participate in trade unions, are entitled to freedom of assembly and speech, have the same equal protection of the laws as do citizens, and in some countries can vote in the local elections. They have the right to remain in the country, even if unemployed and dependent upon public benefits, unless convicted of crimes. The major difference between citizens and noncitizens is in the realm of obligations: noncitizen migrants are not obliged to serve in the military and in the United States they are not called to jury duty.

While these difference are not trivial they have ceased to loom very large in the everyday life of most migrants. Expulsion of legal residents is uncommon. The lack of voting rights is viewed by migrants as of little importance, especially since migrants can participate in political affairs at the local level and in trade unions and have access to social welfare benefits. There is considerable evidence that the desire for citizenship is not on the list of concerns of most migrants. Public opinion surveys of Turks and Yugoslavs in West Germany report that migrants have little desire to claim German citizenship and only a small proportion of those eligible for citizenship apply for naturalization. In Switzerland, the European country with the largest proportion of migrant workers, migrants do not clamor for citizenship, though it is even more difficult to obtain citizenship than in Germany. France permits its migrants to naturalize, but there are few takers. The annual naturalization rate, though higher than that of Switzerland and Germany, remains well below that of the United States, Canada, and Australia. Even in these latter countries, large numbers of migrants choose not to become citizens although in all three countries the acquisition of citizenship is easy. Many migrants, no matter how long they stay abroad, hope to return some day to their native country and are therefore reluctant to change their citizenship.

Migrants who become naturalized citizens do so not because there are significant rights and benefits to be gained but because they wish to assert their membership in and loyalty to the country in which they now live. Studies of the naturalization process in the United States and Australia suggest that the greater the difference between the migrant's culture and that of the host society, the more likely the migrant will seek citizenship: in both countries Asians have a high rate of naturalization, while English-speaking migrants to Australia, and Latins in the United States have a lower naturalization rate. Naturalization is thus part of a process of breaking away from one's roots and reestablishing new ones. For this reason migrants often go through considerable anguish in deciding whether or not to seek citizenship. Old allegiances must be surrendered, new identities formed, and new obligations are incurred, while the gains in rights and benefits are small. (On the naturalization process see Pachon, 1987; North, 1987; Alvarez, 1987; DeSipio, 1987; and Portes and Curtis, 1987; on the issue of cultural gains and losses for migrants, see Shils in McNeill and Adams, 1978.)

With the incorporation of immigrants in liberal democracies, citizenship as a means of acquiring rights and benefits has diminished in importance while citizenship as a set of obligations and allegiances retains its central significance. For this reason it is immigration policy rather than naturalization policy that is the point of contention for immigrants and potential immigrants.

This is not to suggest that the issue of citizenship for migrants and their children is of no importance. It is of importance to liberal democrats that millions of people permanently living in Western Europe cannot vote, and regard themselves and are regarded by citizens as outsiders. The question of whether to incorporate migrants into society is not an issue in historical immigrant countries such as the United States and Canada, where naturalization is relatively easy and where sufficient cultural pluralism exists so that migrants can naturalize or change their political allegiance without surrendering their personal cultural identity; it is more of an issue in those European countries which make naturalization difficult and which make citizenship identical with cultural identity. The danger in these societies is that migrants and their children become permanent residents, but either by exclusion or by choice do not become citizens, and remain economically marginalized and culturally on the periphery.

Countries that make naturalization difficult and which do not automatically make the locally born children of migrants citizens are in danger of developing social systems in which class and ethnic divisions coincide. The extension of citizenship to the migrants and especially to their children is a first minimal step toward incorporation, for it helps to establish allegiances and obligations among the migrants and commits the state and the society toward full civic equality. The extension of citizenship to migrants does not ensure that an ethnic division of labor among some migrant groups will not develop. But it is an essential step, for if large numbers of migrants and their descendants do not become citizens, then liberal democracies are in danger of becoming two-tiered societies in which those who are citizens regard those who are not as outside the civic society, unworthy of social respect, disdained for the work they do, and regarded as unwelcome guests. Under such circumstances the xenophobic tendency that is inherent in all homogeneous societies will be reinforced.

BIBLIOGRAPHY

Alvarez, Robert R. "A Profile of the Citizenship Process Among Hispanics in the United States." *International Migration Review*, vol 21, no. 2:327-347.

Bennett, Douglas C. "Immigration, Work and Citizenship in the American Welfare State." Paper presented at the 1986 Annual Meeting of the American Political Science Association, Washington, D.C. August 1986.

Brown, Colin. "Ethnic Pluralism in Britain: the Demographic and Legal Background" in *Ethnic Pluralism and Public Policy*, edited by Nathan Glazer and Ken Young, 32-53. Lexington: Mass: Lexington Books, D.C. Heath and Company.

Brubaker, William Rogers, ed. *Immigration and the Politics of Citizenship in Europe and North America*. Lanham: University Press of America, 1989.

————. "Immigration and the Politics of Citizenship in Late Nineteenth Century France," Society of Fellows, Harvard University, 1989.

Carens, Joseph H. "Aliens and Citizens: The Case for Open Borders," *The Review of Politics*, 49, no. 2 (Spring 1987), 251-271.

—————."Immigration and the Welfare State" in *Democracy and the Welfare State,* edited by Amy Gutmann, 207-230. Princeton: Princeton University Press.

—————."Membership and Morality: Admission to Citizenship in Liberal Demoratic States" in *Immigration and the Politics of Citizenship in Europe and North America,* edited by William Rogers Brubaker, *op. cit.,* 31-49.

—————."Nationalism and the Exclusion of Immigrants: Lessons from Australian Immigration Policy" in *Open Borders? Closed Societies? The Ethical and Political Issues,* edited by Mark Gibney, 41-60. New York: Greenwood Press.

Crewe, Ivor. "Representation and the Ethnic Minorities in Britain" in *Ethnic Pluralism and Public Policy: Achieving Equality in the United States and Britain,* edited by Nathan Glazer and Ken Young, 258-300. Lexington: Lexington Books, D.C. Heath and Company.

DeSipio, Louis. "Social Science Literature and the Naturalization Process," *International Migration Review,* vol. 21, no. 2: 390-405.

Easterlin, Richard A., David Ward, William S. Bernard, Reed Ueda. *Immigration,* chapter 4, "Naturalization and Citizenship," 106-159. Cambridge: Harvard University Press, 1982,

Evans, M.D.R. "Choosing to be a Citizen: The Time-Path of Citizenship in Australia." *International Migration Review,* vol 21, no. 2 (1987), 243-364.

Gordon, Linda W. "Asian Immigration Since World War II" in *Immigration and U.S. Foreign Policy,* edited by Robert W. Tucker, Charles B. Keely, and Linda Wrigley, 169-191. Boulder: Westview Press, 1990.

Hailbronner, Kay. "Citizenship and Nationhood in Germany" in *Immigration and the Politics of Citizenship in Europe and North America,* edited by William Rogers Brubaker, *op. cit.,* 81-96.

Hammar, Tomas, editor. *European Immigration Policy: A Comparative Study.* Cambridge: Cambridge University Press, 1985.

—————."Citizenship, Aliens' Political Rights, and Politicians' Concern for Migrants: The Case of Sweden" in *Guests Come to Stay: The Effects of European Labor Migration in Sending and Receiving Countries,* edited by Rosemarie Rogers, 85-107. Boulder: Westview Press, 1985.

Hoffmann-Nowotny, Hans Joachim. "Switzerland" in *European Immigration Policy: A Comparative Study,* edited by Tomas Hammar, 206-235. Cambridge: Cambridge University Press, 1985.

Horowitz, Donald L. "Europe and America: A Comparative Analysis of Ethnicity." *Revue Europeene des Migrations Internationales,* vol. 5, no. 1 (1989): 47-59.

Layton-Henry, Zig. "Great Britain" in *European Immigration Policy: A Comparative Study,* edited by Thomas Hammar, 89-126. Cambridge: Cambridge University Press, 1985.

Mayo Smith, Richmond. *Emigration and Immigration: A Study in Social Science.* New York: Charles Scribner's Sons, 1890, Johnson Reprint Corporation, New York, 1968.

Miller, Mark J. "Dual Citizenship: A European Norm?" *International Migration Review,* vol. 23, no. 4, 1989: 945-950.

North, David S. "The Long Grey Welcome: A Study of the American Naturalization Program." *International Migration Review*, vol. 21, no. 2 (1987): 311-326.

Pachon, Harry P. "Naturalization: Determinants and Process in the Hispanic Community: An Overview of Citizenship in the Hispanic Community." *International Migration Review*, vol 21, no. 2 (1987): 299-310.

Peters, B. Guy and Patricia K. Davis. "Migration to the United Kingdom and the Emergence of a New Politics," *Annals*, AAPSS, 485 (May 1986): 129-138.

Plender, Richard. *International Migration Law*. Leiden: A.W. Sijthoff, 1972.

Portes, Alejandro and John W. Curtis. "Changing Flags: Naturalization and its Determinants Among Mexican Migrants," *International Migration Review*, vol. 21, no. 2 (1987): 352-371.

Price, Charles. "Australia" in *The Politics of Migration Policies*, edited by Daniel Kubat. New York: Basic Books, 1973.

Rawls, John. *A Theory of Justice*. Cambridge, Mass: Harvard University Press, 1971.

Rogers, Rosemarie. "The Transnational Nexus of Migration." *Annals*, AAPSS, 485 (May 1986): 34-50.

Scanlan, John A., and O.T. Kent. "The Force of Moral Arguments for a Just Immigration Policy in a Hobbesian Universe: The Contemporary American Example" in *Open Borders? Closed Societies? The Ethical and Political Issues*, edited by Mark Gibney, 61-107. New York: Greenwood Press.

Schuck, Peter H., and Rogers M. Smith. *Citizenship with Consent: Illegal Aliens in the American Polity*. New Haven: Yale University Press, 1985.

──────."Immigration Law and the Problem of Community" in *Clamor at the Gates: The New American Immigration*, edited by Nathan Glazer. San Francisco: ICS Press, 1985: 285-307

Shils, Edward. "Root—The Sense of Place and Past: The Cultural Gains and Losses of Migration" in *Human Migration Patterns and Policies*, edited by William H. McNeill and Ruth S. Adams. Bloomington: Indiana University Press, 1978: 404-426.

Shimada, Haruo. "A Possible Solution to the Problem of Foreign Labor," *Japan Review of International Affairs*, vol. 4, no. 1 (1990): 66-90.

Walzer, Michael. *Spheres of Justice: A Defense of Pluralism and Equality*, New York: Basic Books, 1983.

Weiner, Myron. "International Migration and Development: Indians in the Persian Gulf." *Population and Development Review*, vol. 8, no. 1 (1982): 1-36.

──────."On International Migration and International Relations" in *Population and Development Review*, vol. 11, no. 3 (1985): 441-455.

Whelan, Frederick G., "Citizenship and Freedom of Movement: An Open Admission Policy?" in *Open Borders? Closed Societies? The Ethnical and Political Issues*, edited by Mark Gibney. New York: Greenwood Press, 3-39

Index

A

aborigines, 120
academics, 54
accident insurance, 112, 138
Acheson, Dean, 117
Adelson, Joseph, 105, 111
adolescents, 13, 105-106, 109
adversarialism, 89-90
affluence, 5, 98-99, 108-110
African population, 118
age, 52, 72, 74, 96-97, 101, 112, 136,
    138, 140
agitators, 5
Aid to Dependent Children, 136
airport controllers, 12
alcohol, 100-101, 103
Algeria, 122, 140
Algerian FLN, 124
alphabet, 102
Alsace-Lorraine, 122
altruism, altruistic, 2, 27
American Civil Liberties Union, 51
American Founding, 57, 59-61, 63,
    65-67, 69, 71-73, 153
American Sunday School Union, 100
Amsterdam (see also Netherlands), 96
anarchy, anarchic license, 20, 47, 84,
    126
ancestry, 52
anger, 57
antagonists, 4, 11
anthropology, 10, 103, 120
anti-slavery movements, 100
Aquinas, Thomas, 18
Arab population, 118, 122, 145
arbitrariness, 34, 92, 128
Arcadia (see also Canada), 98
Arendt, Hannah, 20, 29, 34, 37-38
aristocracy, 10-11, 93, 100
Aristophanes, 78
Aristotle, 18, 20, 44, 46, 54-56, 59, 61,
    66, 73, 101, 111

Armenia, 50
arrest rate, 97
art, 29, 60
Asia, 117, 127, 130-131, 135, 141, 145
Asian Americans, 108
assaults, 95
Assistant Secretary of State for the Near
    East, South Asia and Africa, 117
Athens (see also Greece), 66, 77-78
audacity, 28
Australia, 130-133, 141-144, 147-151
Austro-Hungarian Empire, 116
authenticity, 92
auto theft, 96
Azerbajianis, 50

B

baby boom generation, 96
bad manners, 60
Bahrain, 145
balance of power, 25, 115-116
Bandung (see also Indonesia), 116-117,
    119, 123
Bandung Conference, 117, 119, 123
barbarians, 58
bargaining, 8
Bay of Bengal, 118
beasts, 63
begging, 34
Belfast (see also Ireland, Northern), 96,
    98
Belgium, 116
Bellah, Robert, 59
Bible (see also Scripture), 69, 100
biblical revelation, 60
bigot, 50
Bill of Rights, 40, 52, 71, 129
blacks, 13, 38, 42, 50, 107-108, 112, 153
Bloom, Allan, 93, 151
Boer War, 121
Bolshevism, 121, 124
Bombay (see also India), 98